Unlearning

or
'How NOT To Be Governed?'

A Crucial 'Capability' for 'Education-as-*Paideia*'
and a 'Democracy to Come'

Nader N. Chokr

SOCIETAS

essays in political
& cultural criticism

imprint-academic.com

Published in the UK by Societas
Imprint Academic, PO Box 200, Exeter EX5 5YX, UK

Published in the USA by Societas
Imprint Academic, Philosophy Documentation Center
PO Box 7147, Charlottesville, VA 22906-7147, USA

ISBN 9781845401641

A CIP catalogue record for this book is available from the
British Library and US Library of Congress

Contents

'The philosopher's task: to harm stupidity.'
« La tache du philosophe : nuire a la bêtise »

(Nietzsche, *Gay Science* IV #328)

'I would thus propose this general characterization as a rather preliminary definition of critique: the art of not being governed so much.'

(Michel Foucault, *What is Critique?*)

Preface

This essay is based on an idea first articulated during an Inter-disciplinary University-wide Seminar on 'The Capabilities Approach' at Shandong University (Jinan, China) during the Fall semester of 2006. A much shorter version was prepared for the purpose of the 19th International Conference of the International Association of Greek Philosophy (IAGP) on the theme 'Education in the Global Era' in Samos, Greece, July 15–21, 2007.

The first complete version of this project was produced by December 2007, and revised with an added postscript in July 2008 (shortly before my departure from China to Oslo, Norway where I now reside). All subsequent revisions since then consisted of minor corrections and refinements rather than substantive changes. As always, I am thankful to Li Xiaolin for her interest in the ideals and values upheld herein, and for prodding me to develop and complete this project, which has remained far too long in gestation on the 'back-burner'.

The initial hypotheses and provisional conclusions of my inquiry into the issues discussed herein were presented in part and discussed during 'my last Seminar' in China (September 2007–January 2008) at Shandong University. It was held every Thursday afternoon from 2 to 6 pm within the intimate secrecy of my office at the School of Philosophy and Social Development. At long last, I was finally able to lead a Seminar in Contemporary Philosophy in China that was fully engaged and engaging, that upheld the kind of educational values I have come to believe in, and that I defend herein.

It is with regret however, and a great sadness in my heart, that I must also mention the following fact, or should I say, to use a dedicated Chinese expression 'teaching accident': I was unfortunately compelled to cancel the Seminar before the end of the semester because I had suddenly and by arbitrary decree lost my position as Professor of Philosophy & Social Sciences at Shandong University, a position that I had held for the past 4 years. This is all the more puzzling and disturbing as I was, so I was told (I never checked), the first foreign philosophy professor (US citizen) to have been appointed full-time at a Chinese University since the so-called 'opening'.

I hope to have the opportunity some day soon to tell the detailed story of this misadventure, or rather shameful debacle, in another context. For now, I would like to thank all the participants for the lively discussions, intense inquiries, and radical questioning that they willingly and joyfully engaged in during the Seminar while it lasted. They had come literally from all four corners of the world, and had all found themselves in my Seminar along with my Chinese students in a totally contingent manner. What they all seemed to have in common was an itch to probe deeper and go further in their critical thinking about the problems and issues of our times.

Following the cancellation of my Seminar, some among them undertook to translate the English text of my essay into French and Chinese respectively. I am most grateful for their hard work and determination in producing these translations, which are also scheduled for publication. I am most grateful, in particular, to Hermann Aubie, one of the participants and among the most engaged contributors, and currently a PhD candidate in Comparative Literature at the University of Rennes 2 (France), for his careful work on the French translation. I also would like to thank Chen Xiaoxu, one of my former students, currently a PhD candidate in Philosophy at Cambridge University, for undertaking the radical revision and refinement of the preliminary translation into Chinese completed earlier by Fang Zhen and some of my other graduate students at Shandong University (Shuedan, Li Chao, Zhang Meng, Liu Xiuming, and I must be forgetting other names). To all, I am equally grateful for their respective efforts and contributions.

My aim in this essay is to show why we should hold 'unlearning' to be a crucial 'capability' *in* and *for* education at this point in our history. Essentially, I argue that it enables to pose and take seriously the problem of 'governmentality': How are we governed—individually and collectively? Do we wish to be governed in this or that way, to this or that extent, so much, so little, or so badly, under these or those conditions? Or do we wish instead to be self-governed and thereby practice our freedom and be more autonomous, relatively speaking? As such, it puts in question in a radical way the twin pillars of the so-called 'contemporary consensus'—'representative (liberal or social) democracy' and 'capitalism'—and makes it possible to take a critical measure of their limits, insufficiencies, and irremediable deficits. Only an unmitigated advocacy of 'unlearning' can bring about a paradigm shift that can move us from the present system of (mis)education as it evolved in modernity and postmodernity to education-as-*paideia* in the 21st century. Inscribed within a redefined transitional politics of resistance and autonomy, and a framework for emancipatory education, it furthermore enables us to envision and apprehend properly the normative connections between education-as-*paideia*, critical and self-reflective citizenship, 'democracy to come' (or radical and inclusive democracy), and social justice. Such a conception is under-written and supported by a critical role for a (reconceived and transformed) philosophy, after the end of Philosophy, whose main task, if it is still to be relevant today, ought to be 'mediocrity-and-bullshit' detection and busting.

Oslo, Norway
October 2008

Unlearning or 'How NOT to be Governed?'

Prelude

We need not be condemned to the festive dereliction of 'the last men' celebrating their inability and impotence to govern themselves even while they naively believe to have reached finally a comfortable harbor of certainty. We need not be condemned, without hope of recourse, to the motionless frenzy and perpetual agony of the living-dead of post-history. History must go on — because the end is in fact always a new beginning. And the single most pressing question confronting us is therefore this: how are we going 'to make history', or rather, how will we choose 'to inhabit history'? — What is going to be the form of the 'democracy to come'? What kind of 'education' can best help in bringing it about?

1. Against the Tradition: Unlearning vs. Learning

Even though 'education' has been conceived differently at different periods in history — with different emphases, priorities, strategies and goals — it has invariably been defined across cultures in terms of 'learning'. Otherwise, it has been characterized in terms of what 'learned *men*'[1] for the most part (those who have presumably acquired and mastered 'learning' and who therefore are said to possess 'knowledge'[2]) deem desirable and worthwhile enough on behalf of the dominant groups or ruling elites of their respective societies. Whatever they deem to be so is then included as part of the long and arduous transmission process, without which no society can endure and reproduce itself over time. Such a process typically involves passing on to younger generations some specific knowledge-contents (validated within a given dominant epistemic framework), as well as various useful and practical, basic skills and abilities of various kinds, commensurate with different phases or stages of development.

Right from the start, it is, I believe, useful to note (if only parenthetically) Foucault's distinction between 'dominant knowledge' (*savoirs dominants*) and 'subjugated knowledge' (*savoirs subjugués*) which is applicable to any society at any given moment of its history. A given framework for knowledge is established as dominant by relegating to the

---

[1]   I am here alluding to the *sexist* and *patriarchal* dominance in education particularly and culture more generally, and throughout the ages in almost all major societies and cultures around the world—even though there were quite a few *learned women* across cultures. One should also note the questionable *political* and *ethnocentric* dimensions of education that such a formulation implies. In any case, the ideal of education has traditionally been becoming 'a learned man'—whether it be in the mythical ancient 'West' or 'East'.

[2]   This clearly suggests a 'property-based model of knowledge', that is validated according to the 'dominant social paradigm'. By the latter, I mean 'the system of beliefs, ideas and corresponding values which are dominant (or tend to become dominant) in a particular society at a particular moment of its history, and which are "most consistent" with the existing political, economic and social institutions' (see further discussion in section 4).

dustbin of history and oblivion a number of other, alternative, and 'subjugated' 'ways of knowing'. By *subjugated
knowledges'*, Foucault means a whole set of knowledges that
are either hidden behind more dominant knowledges but
can be revealed through *critique* or have been explicitly
disqualified as inadequate to their task or insufficiently
elaborated: for example, 'naïve knowledges', located low
down on the hierarchy, beneath the required level of cogni-
tion or scientificity (Foucault, 1980, p. 82). [Note the
unusual plural use of 'knowledge' which is due to the fact
that the French have two words for it, and draw a distinction between *'connaissance'* and *'savoir'* (O'Farrell, 2005,
pp. 7 and 142).]

It is arguably commonly drawn in hermeneutics, as well
as in non-Latin languages. In English for example, a distinction is made between 'formal knowledge' and 'tacit or
informal knowledge' or between 'know-that' and
'know-how. Similarly, the German distinguish between
'wissenshaftliches Wissen' and *'Erfahrungswissen'* or
'lebensweltliches Wissen'. Obviously, they have something to
do with each other; however, they are also produced and
related to each other differently at different periods of
history.

For our present purpose, we might hold that 'knowl-
edge-as-*connaissance'* refers to an *object*; it is transitive,
'objective' whereas 'knowledge-as-*savoir'* refers somehow
to the capacity of a living *subject*. The latter consists always
in 'know-how', 'know-how-to-act', 'know-how-to-commu-
nicate', 'know-how-to-behave', in short, various abilities
and habits stemming for the most part from a corporeal
intelligence and intuition. It is typically difficult to translate
into words and formulas. It is acquired by experience, by
the fact of being immersed in surrounding interactions and
activities. In contrast, 'knowledge-as-*connaissance'* is more

of the order of logical or formal thought; it is knowledge of the laws and relations; its operations, processes and procedures, can all essentially be transcribed into formal, information-software language. In this context, it might worth asking ourselves in passing what is really meant by the emergence of the so-called 'knowledge society or economy' in this latest phase of the post-industrial development of global capitalism.

Elsewhere, Foucault states:

> When I say 'subjugated knowledges' I mean two things. On the one hand, I am referring to historical contents that have been buried or masked in functional coherences or formal systematizations. In other words, I am referring to blocks of historical knowledges that were present in the functional and systematic ensembles, but which were masked, and the *critique* was able to reveal their existence by using, obviously enough, the tools of scholarship. On the other hand (...), I am also referring to a whole series of knowledges that have been disqualified as (...) insufficiently elaborated (...): naïve knowledges, hierarchically inferior knowledges, (...) that are below the required level of erudition and scientificity (Foucault, 2003, p. 7).

Against this traditional, entrenched way of thinking about 'education', I would like to argue that the concept of *'un-learning'* is more appropriate for what education should require today if it is to have an emancipatory role. Such a role is itself called for by the historical conditions that we are confronted with at this juncture of our history, namely, the 'rising tide of mediocrity-and-bullshit'.[3] This is in any case what I will contend by the close of this essay.

---

[3]   See Chokr, *An Archeology of Mediocrity – A Contribution to the Analysis of the Emergence of a New Form of 'Fascism'* (2009), forthcoming. See also Ahmed's recent article 'Mass Mentality, Culture Industry, and Fascism' (2008, pp. 79–94).

In the meantime, and parenthetically, it might suffice to note my working hypothesis. There is, I believe, a mutually sustaining relationship between 'mediocrity' and 'bullshit': one leads to the other and vice-versa. By 'mediocrity', on the one hand, I mean something other than what is commonly understood by this term. I mean to suggest instead a number of converging socio-cultural-political processes by which the drive toward the 'lowest common denominator' is reaching a new high. This is leading to the uniformization and homogenization of minds and bodies, the absence of (critical) thinking, and the dummification of people not only at the macro-level, but more insidiously, at the micro-physical and micro-physiological level of the social fabric and the body politic. Such processes are arguably contributing to the emergence of 'a new form of fascism', i.e., a fascism that is different in its manifestations and modes of operation for the ones we experienced during the 20th century. For this reason, a proper understanding of how it works and a proper assessment of its impact require new analytical tools, aimed most specifically at the micro-physical and micro-physiological levels, where it seems most efficacious because it is for the most part 'invisible' and 'undetectable'. Counteracting and fighting its hegemony calls for a radical politics of resistance and autonomy.

By 'bullshit', on the other hand, I am referring to the pervasive phenomenon characteristic of our times, which has been aptly though partially discussed in a groundbreaking study by Harry Frankfurt (1988/2005).[4] Though, like pornography, the obscenity of 'bullshit' may be hard to define in a strict manner, everybody knows what it is when

---

[4]   See also Chokr (2006) for a critical discussion of his view as well as that of G. A. Cohen (2002).

confronted with it, or subjected to it. It is unquestionably happening across the board in almost all areas of activity and spheres of our personal and public life. Besides, there are many different forms and degrees of 'bullshit' relative to different domains and areas, and new forms and variations are being produced continuously every day. One can only marvel in awe and shock in the face of the creativity of our 'achievements' in this regard: truly historic!

Under the view advocated here, education should above all consist in *'learning how to learn independently'*, and eventually, if need be, in *unlearning*. The former is arguably not even possible in any meaningful and substantive way without the latter, and the latter is stronger and far more demanding than what is usually meant by 'critical thinking'. Besides, as I will argue in the final analysis, it calls for a new and reconceived role for philosophy — after the end of Philosophy.

The term which captures best what I mean by 'unlearning' is perhaps Foucault's notion of *'se deprendre'*, which, I believe, presupposes something like *'désapprendre'* (which means literally 'to unlearn'). It is still unclear to me how to best translate or render the former notion into English. As a preliminary characterization, however, I would say that it consists in being moved by the desire and willful determination *'not to be taken in'*. Ultimately, it is about 'unshackling oneself'. To put it in more familiar terms, it is about 'emancipating' or 'liberating' oneself from variously entrenched and often unquestioned ways of thinking, doing and living by radically questioning, criticizing and rejecting the assumptions and premises of much of what one has learned as part of the 'dominant and established system(s) of knowledge'. As a preliminary definition of 'critique,' Foucault offered the following general characterization: the art of *not* being governed so much ('What is Critique?', in Rabinow and Rose, 1994, p. 265).

I realize that proposing such a goal for education may seem at first rather counter-intuitive and even paradoxical, for it is commonly assumed that education can only be conceived according to the 'banking model', to use Paolo Freire's term (1970), and can only consist in learning, acquiring, possessing, and accumulating 'knowledge-content' of some kind. I hope, however, to be able to clarify my position in due course, or in any case, to make it seem less counter-intuitive and less paradoxical, and therefore more plausible.

In the meantime, it may be helpful to take note of a fundamental assumption underwriting this analysis — which stems from its debt to the legacy of the Enlightenment. It is obviously always preferable to rationally scrutinize and question any knowledge presented to us than to accept it merely on faith, or on the basis of authority, because it is said to be so. In addition, and most importantly however, it is arguably urgent for us to reconsider our ever-expanding drive toward knowledge and always more knowledge, as an end in itself, and recognize the necessity to keep at the forefront of our considerations and deliberations the most crucial, ethical question: 'knowledge for what? — in order to achieve which goals, purposes, or ends?' This line of thinking is directly inscribed within the broader ethical concern underlying this essay: How should I/we live? How should we make the world a more humane and livable place?

By most assessments of the history of Modernity and Postmodernity, we have been led to live today in a world dominated by 'the tyranny of instrumental-cognitive reason' — of which 'mercantile reason' and 'economic reason' are only two instantiations. This was the result of the dark unfolding of the Dialectic of the Enlightenment, in which the 'practical and pragmatic reason of ends' seems to have been relegated to the sidelines or even to the benches. We have more and more knowledge, more and more scientific and technological power, and 'the world of technology' so dreaded by earlier philosophers such as Heidegger is now upon us. And yet it is clear that we still don't know how to live together, nor do we have a more humane and habitable world. The opposite is in fact true. Far from having a clear vision of where we should be going, of our priorities and goals, we seem to be far less capable of even entertaining such a scenario. One thing seems clearer everyday, we are everyday nearer to the disaster and catastrophe that will send the world, as we know it, twirling into the chaos of self-inflicted destruction and devastation on a scale so far unseen and unimaginable.

In view of such a diagnosis, how can we then begin to recreate the necessary conditions for a rehabilitation of 'practical reason'? A reason for which 'pure or theoretical reason' is only one possible instance and exemplification, and to which 'instrumental-cognitive reason' would be subordinated, i.e., the 'practical, ethical, aesthetic, or pragmatic reason of ends'. How can we best refocus our attention on its singular importance at this point of our history?

Toward that end, I propose to examine the concept of *unlearning* (in the context of education) and the kinds of questions it invites in light of two crucial, yet apparently disparate contributions — namely those of Amartya Sen and Martha Nussbaum with their concept of '*capability*' and Michel Foucault's with his concept of '*governmentality*'.

To begin with, Sen and Nussbaum are interested in formulating an alternative way for thinking about *well-being*, *quality of life*, *human development*, and ultimately, *social and global justice*. It is one that is, unlike other theories or conceptions of justice, anchored in the concept of 'capability', rather than that of 'resources', 'income', or 'Rawlsian primary goods'. The fundamental intuition underwriting their approach is that certain distinctly human capabilities exert a moral claim upon us that calls forth their further development and expansion — at least beyond a certain threshold.

By 'capability', Sen means the empowering and *substantive* (and not merely formal) *freedom* of an individual agent to choose (or not) to actualize a given *functioning* from within a range of *valuable beings and doings* considered to be necessary and minimal conditions for a truly *flourishing* human life. In contrast, Nussbaum distinguishes three different, yet related kinds of capabilities: basic, internal and combined. The first ones have to do with 'the innate equipment of individuals that is the necessary basis for developing the more advanced capabilities, and a ground for moral concern'. The second ones have to do with the 'developed states of the person herself that are, so far as the person herself is concerned, sufficient conditions for the exercise of requisite functions'; in other words, 'unlike the basic capabilities, these states are mature conditions of readiness'. The third ones are 'defined as internal capabilities *combined with* suitable external conditions for the exercise of the function' (2000, pp. 84–5).

Unlike Sen, who opts for a 'deliberate and assertive incompleteness' on the kinds of capabilities that should be developed, preferring to leave it to each society to make such a determination through deliberative and democratic processes,[5] Nussbaum proposes a provisional list of ten

---

[5]   However, from his writings, and the numerous examples he uses to illustrate his theoretical points, one could easily derive a list of what are, in Sen's view, 'basic or fundamental capabilities and

'central combined capabilities' as part of a partial theory of social justice. She believes that such a list could become the object of an 'overlapping consensus'.[6] She claims that 'such a list gives us the basis for determining a decent social minimum in a variety of areas' and she argues further that 'the structure of social and political institutions should be chosen, at least in part, with a view to promoting at least a threshold level of these human capabilities' (2000, p. 75). Of all the capabilities she lists, she claims that the single most important one is that of *practical reason*, which she defines as 'the ability to form and revise a conception of the good and to engage in critical reflection about the planning of one's life' (2000, p. 79).[7] She adds further: 'To realize one of the items on the list for citizens of a nation entails not only promoting appropriate development of their internal powers, but also preparing the environment so that it is favorable for the exercise of practical reason and the other major functions' (2000, p. 85).

However, nowhere on her list do we find anything remotely close to what I mean by 'unlearning' and that I here contend must be included and for good reasons.[8] One might argue that even though 'unlearning' is not explicitly

---

functionings' as opposed to more 'advanced and refined capabilities and functionings'.

[6]   See Chokr (2007d) for a critical discussion. See also Nussbaum (2000, p. 78–80) for details of her revised list. The 'central combined capabilities' included in her latest, revised list are: (1) Life (2) Bodily Health (3) Bodily Integrity (4) Senses, Imagination, and Thought (5) Emotions (6) Practical Reason (7) Affiliation (8) Other Species (9) Play, and (10) Control over one's (Political and Material) Environment.

[7]   In fairness, I must note that she also considers 'affiliation' to be almost on a par with 'practical reason'.

[8]   This point is also noted duly by Chen Xiaoxu in her thesis — written under my supervision at Shandong University, China: *The Capabilities Approach: Problems and Prospects* (2006, p. 77n2).

included, it could be easily derived given the other provisions typically countenanced by the capabilities approach [i.e., those of 'practical reason' (Nussbaum) and agency (Sen)]. I would be inclined to agree with such reasoning. However, I would add, it needs to be made explicit in order to stress the normative and emancipatory dimension of the approach.[9]

As for Foucault, it is fair to say that much of his work has consisted in analyzing the various manifestations of 'power' and configurations of 'power/knowledge', which, in his view, have characterized and shaped the history of Western culture. He did so, I believe, in an effort to bring out hitherto unsuspected forms of domination and oppression as well as pointing to various possibilities for resistance and autonomy (Chokr, 2007). For this purpose, he articulated and developed a set of successive conceptual tools — such as 'pastoral power', '(political) sovereign power', 'disciplinary power', 'bio-power', and finally that of 'governmentality'. For my present purposes, I will concentrate on the latter notion, and only indirectly discuss these other notions.[10]

---

[9]   For further details on the two main versions of the Capabilities Approach, see Amartya Sen (1984; 1985; 1987; 1992; 1993; 1999b); see also Martha Nussbaum (1988; 1992; 1993; 2000a, 2000b; 2003).

[10]   It may help however to keep in mind the following characterizations. By *'pastoral power'*, Foucault meant to refer to the kind of power exercised by the Church — through its priests and pastors as 'shepherds of the flock of God'. It rests on the Church's power to assure individual salvation in the next world. It is linked with the notion of individualism (as in individual salvation). In modern times however, 'salvation in the next world' is commuted into 'salvation in this life' and now concern itself with the health, well-being, and security of individuals and groups (for details, see Foucault's 1978 lecture on Security, Territory and Population, Rabinow, 1997, pp. 67–71; Dreyfus and Rabinow, 1982, pp. 213–5; O'Farrell, 2005, p. 150). By *'sovereign power'*, Foucault refers to a system of government based squarely on the power of the King (see O'Farrell, 2005, p. 130). By

Foucault came to the notion of 'governmentality' by recognizing the limitations of his previous work and conceptual resources. Instead of restricting freedoms, as did 'disciplinary power', the new notion he proposed allowed for the incorporation of these freedoms into the mechanisms that guide people's behaviours in the social body. In his analyses of bio-power over the life of 'populations', he kept running into the problem of government. He noted that in the 16th century there were a whole series of problems that were centered around the following kinds of questions: how to govern oneself, how to be governed, how to govern

---

'*disciplinary power*', he meant to characterize the kind of power that progressively took over from 'sovereign power' in the 18th and 19th centuries, in a complex interaction between the two forms of powers, and that led the emergence of what Foucault calls a 'disciplinary society'. In such a society, the mechanism of disciplinary power, as one way in which power can be exercised, regulates the behaviour and the body of individuals in the social body. It consists in a form of surveillance that is internalized by individuals. Each person is somehow enrolled in his or her discipline. Its goal is to produce disciplined, normalized, well-functioning, and docile individuals. The emergence of 'disciplinary power' is connected, Foucault contends, with the rise of capitalism. Disciplinary technologies were crucial for producing docile people. Their aim was to forge and produce 'a docile body that may be subjected, used, transformed, and improved' as he shows in *Discipline and Punish*. Without the insertion of disciplined, orderly individuals into the machinery of production, the new demands of capitalism would have been stymied (see O'Farrell, 2005, p. 133; Dreyfus and Rabinow, 1982, p. 134–5). By '*bio-power*' (and the related term of 'bio-politics'), Foucault means to characterize the increasing State concern with the biological well-being of its population including births, deaths, reproduction, illnesses and diseases prevention and control, food and water supply, sanitary shelter, and education. As a coherent political technology, it emerged in the 17th century and was further consolidated by the late 18th century. Basically, it incorporates two components: (1) Scientific categorization and classification of human beings (species, populations, race, gender, sexual practices, etc). This component was also tied up with the practice of confession. (2)

others, by whom will the people accept to be governed, how to become the best possible governor? (Foucault, 1979/1986).

When he first introduced the term in his lectures at the College de France on 'The Birth of Biopolitics' in 1978 (Rabinow, 1997, pp. 73–9), his main concern was with government in the narrow and restricted sense of 'the exercise of political sovereignty'. He explained that he originally meant three things: (1) the institutions and knowledge that serve to manage the population; (2) the pre-eminence of certain exercises of power based on administrative practices of governance; (3) the process by which a State, based on a system on law in the Middle Ages in Europe, was replaced by a way of administering a population. In other words, 'governmentality' was then the *rationalization and systematization of a particular way of exercising political sovereignty through the government of people's conduct*. In Foucault's view, the idea of governing a population rather than simply ruling over a territory is something that started to emerge in Europe in the 16th century, by adopting and adapting aspects and dimensions of 'pastoral power' or pastoral forms of governance. Such power, which already existed in the Church, aimed at saving people's souls.

Even though, like 'disciplinary power' and 'bio-power', 'governmentality' emerged in opposition to 'sovereign forms of power', it did not entirely supersede and cancel out the latter. Sovereign power involved obedience to the law of the sovereign—as a representative of God on earth—and was concerned with ruling over a territory. In contrast,

---

Disciplinary aspects about managing and control populations and individuals in every aspect of their life, leading up to the *management and control of life itself* (see O'Farrell, 2005, p. 130; Foucault, (1997), *History of Sexuality*, 1976/1990, part 5).

government was concerned with all the means for attaining a number of goals, including naturally the wealth and health of the population of the State and the increase of that population, thereby strengthening the power of the State. It was no longer merely a matter of owning and ruling over a territory [see lectures on 'Security, Territory, and Population' in Rabinow (1997, pp. 67–71)].

Over time however the notion of 'governmentality' came to mean not so much the political or administrative structures of the modern State as *all the techniques, technologies, and procedures by which the conduct of individuals or of populations might be guided and governed at every level and in every aspect.* Foucault often cited the following examples: the government of children, of souls and consciences, of communities, of families, of the sick, of the mentally ill, of the marginal and criminal elements in society, of the state, or of oneself, etc. To govern, in this sense, is *to structure the possible field of action of others.*

Though Foucault also used this notion to characterize the centralization and increase of government power, he did not view this power as being necessarily negative. For him, it could also be productive.[11] In fact, as he often argued, it

---

[11] I don't mean to assume and validate wholesale and uncritically Foucault's conception of power. However, I do want to avail myself of his 'analytics of power' in that it is different from previous conceptions in which power is almost viewed in macro-logical terms, as operating vertically (top-down) and negatively (as a manifestation of domination — e.g., of the State and its apparatuses). We stand to gain some valuable insights if we were to view it as well, as Foucault suggests, namely, as operating horizontally, in an micro-logical manner or in a bottom-up manner, and across the whole social fabric and body politic. In such a case, it is manifest in all social relationships and could involve resistance, emancipation, liberation, or creation, and thus be productive rather than being merely oppressive and a manifestation of domination. There can be 'no final

produces reality through 'truth-games' and it creates a particular kind of subjectivity to which individuals are expected to conform or that they may choose to resist. However, because individuals are somehow *taken in* by this constructed or constituted subjectivity, they become part of the normalizing force. Largely, people (individuals and groups) internalized this. In addition, discipline, surveillance, and reinforcement of conformity to the rules played their part in bringing about a form of 'voluntary servitude' (as the French philosopher La Boetie would say) in which individuals and groups are enrolled as willing and unsuspecting accomplices in their own subjugation and enslavement.

Thus, 'governmentality' also included a growing body of knowledge that presents itself as 'scientific' and 'objective' and contributes to its power. This was made possible through the creation of specific (expert or professional) 'knowledges' as well as the constitution of 'experts', institutions, and disciplines (e.g., medicine, psychology, psychiatry, criminology, economics, bio-politics, education theory and pedagogy, etc). Hence, the so-called 'experts' could then claim to have the knowledge necessary to wield the power of governmentality.

Toward the end of his life however, Foucault began to move away increasingly from an analysis of the government of the general social body and of 'populations' towards considerations of how individual subjects were governed and (could) govern themselves. In effect, he broadened the scope of 'governmentality' to include all

resolution' of the question of 'power' and it is pointless to continue hoping for one in the form of an ultimate 'liberation' (see Chokr, 2002; 2004b).

forms and techniques of the government of both individuals and groups. His lectures at the College de France in 1980 ('The Government of the Living') and in 1983 ('The Government of the Self and Others') attest to this significant development and change. It is in this context that we must take the transition from his interest in power as it operates at a general level in the social body and body politic to a more pronounced focus on the relation between the subject and truth, and more specifically, a focus on how the subject governs itself, and is governed by others.[12]

Because 'education' is *always already* in some sense a form of indoctrination — so, I contend in any case (Chokr, 2007b), I argue that the only way in which it is worthwhile pursuing is that it be conceived and made so as to give young individuals as well as adult citizens one crucial capability.[13] And that is, the capability to address by themselves the central, incontrovertible and inescapable political question that any properly educated person today (Chokr, 2004) must pose to any social measure, political or economic program or policy, namely, the question of governmentality. How are we governed in our minds and bodies, in our ways of thinking and judging, in our behaviours and actions? Do we wish (or not) to be governed in this or that way, to this or that extent,

---

[12]   For details, see Foucault (1979/1986; 1981; 1982; 1984; 1989 and esp., 2001); Rabinow (1997, pp. 67–71, 73–9, 81–5, and 300); Dreyfus & Rabinow (1982, p. 221); Burchell *et al* (1991); Smart (1992, pp. 559–60); Bratich *et al* (2003); O'Farrell (2005, pp. 106–8, 138).

[13]   Naturally, in addition to all the useful and relevant 'knowledge, skills, and abilities' (KSAs) they need to acquire and make their own in a distinctive and creative way so as to function effectively as deliberating, participating, productive, and meaningfully contributing members in an otherwise justly, well-ordered, and radically democratic and inclusive society. I will argue later on that the forms and modalities of imparting such KSAs must be radically different in the aftermath of the paradigm shift advocated and urged here.

so much, so little, or more to the point, so badly, under these or those (more or less acceptable) conditions (of our own making or not)? Or do we want to be self-governed and autonomous? Should there even be 'government' (in the traditional sense) at all? In some sense, I am prepared to argue that all of education should be conceived in fact in terms of 'capabilities' and 'governmentality'.[14]

This essay is essentially motivated by the desire to explore the possibility of conceiving of 'education' in an emancipatory sense as a precondition for a 'democracy to come' (to use Derrida's expression)—e.g., for a form of 'radical or inclusive democracy' of the kind which has yet to materialize in history,[15] and which in turn presupposes in a strong and meaningful sense critical, self-reflective, engaged and participating citizens. As such, my inquiry is inscribed within a long philosophical tradition, which assumes that there is an intrinsic relationship between 'education', 'citizenship', and 'democracy'—even though these

---

[14] See for example Nussbaum's argument to this effect in her 'Education and Democratic Citizenship: Capabilities and Quality Education' (2006).

[15] The 'democracy to come' project includes a number of protagonists, most notably Derrida (1994; 1997; 2005), Rorty (1983; 1989; 1996; 1998a/b; 1999), Mouffe (1988; 1990; 1992a; 1992b), Laclau and Mouffe (1985), Laclau (1988) as well as Castoriadis (1991; 1997), Fotopoulos (1997; 2003; 2005), and Gorz (1983; 1991; 1997; 2003). While some use the expression 'democracy to come' (Derrida), others prefer to talk about 'postmodern bourgeois liberal democracy' (Rorty), 'radical (plural) democracy' (Mouffe, Laclau, Gorz), or 'inclusive democracy' (Castoriadis, Fotopoulos). It is important to stress the divergent and sometimes conflicting conceptions of 'democracy' that these different authors advocate. For an insightful discussion of Rorty, Mouffe, and Derrida in their efforts to rethinking the democratic project, see Mummery (2005); see also Hekman (1996) for a critical evaluation of the radical plural democracy platform.

concepts have been apprehended and characterized differently by different authors and protagonists.[16]

These concepts can be taken in a descriptive or normative sense. For the most part, I will take them herein in a normative sense, and I distinguish them from their possible (ideological) distortions, misconceptions, and (normative) shortcomings on the basis of their respective *consequences* and *effects* on people's lives — individually and collectively. Whenever they are used descriptively however, it will be to register their failures, deficits, deficiencies, or insufficiencies — despite claims to the contrary by the 'guardians of the *status quo*' and their 'vigilant intellectual clerks', whose critical thinking and unlearning abilities seems to be limited or seriously impaired.

My aim is to show why 'unlearning' — a significant component of 'emancipatory education' within a transitional politics of resistance and autonomy, and therefore, as a precondition for what the Greeks long ago called '*paideia*'[17] — should be viewed as a crucial 'capability' at this juncture of our history. I will contend that it is a capability which enables us to confront head-on the problem of governmentality, and more specifically, to reconsider the connections between emancipatory education, critical and self-reflective citizenship, 'democracy to come' (or radical and inclusive democracy), and social justice from a normative standpoint.

In due course (section 7), I intend to revisit Plato's *Allegory of Cave*, and propose a deconstructive reading or strong

---

[16]   See for example Dewey (1916; 1937); Rorty (1979; 1991); Tarrant (1989); Puolimatka (1995); Nussbaum (2006).

[17]   For a working definition, see forthcoming section in which I provide some etymological, terminological, and conceptual clarifications for the purpose at hand.

misreading in an effort to articulate a number of successive approximations of the meaning of 'unlearning' — in relation to *paideia*.

I take my starting point from the inescapable realization about the poverty and even outright bankruptcy of the present systems of education as they evolved through Modernity and Postmodernity.[18] I will here assume what a properly conducted genealogical inquiry into the emergence of the present system of 'education' would reveal. It would start, say, from the 16th–17th centuries, when the idea of the 'nation-state' was taking shape and gaining ground, move on through the 18th–19th centuries, to consider and examine the shift to liberal (democratic and capitalist) modernity and its corresponding form of 'governmentality'. It would then examine the 20th century, during which we witnessed the emergence of statist or auto-cratic modernity and its corresponding (socialist and com-munist) form of 'governmentality'. Finally, it would deal with our present times, in view of the onslaught of the neo-liberal (post)modernity and its corresponding 'governmentality' along with the emergence of the so-called 'knowledge economy or society' and 'marketplace of education'. In the aftermath of the so-called 'end of ideol-ogies', which has not happened obviously, despite dis-claimers to the contrary, we seem to have entered instead into an era characterized by a single dominant ideology —'representative democracy-cum-capitalism'. Under this ideology, we are witnessing a massive and apparently irre-

---

[18] It makes no difference to my analysis whether a strict distinction can be drawn (or not) between these terms. For my purpose, it suffices to regard 'postmodernity' as a radically critical response to some aspects or elements of Modernity from within Modernity itself, and with the critical resources of Modernity.

pressible encroachment of business and corporate interests on what passes for 'education' — arguably, a grossly negligent form of '(mis)education'. [For a brief genealogical history of the kind that is here assumed to be possible, see Fotopoulos (2003; 2005).]

This leads me subsequently to a radical questioning of the twin pillars of the so-called 'contemporary consensus', according to which we can do no better than 'representative (liberal or social) democracy' coupled with its so-called 'natural ally and complement', 'capitalism'.

The reason why I prefer to talk here about 'capitalism' rather than 'market economy' is that the objections one could raise against the former do not necessarily apply to the latter, without further qualification. As Amartya Sen (1999b) has forcefully argued, 'a market economy' can be efficient, a source of great and desirable productivity, and even a guarantor of substantial freedoms — especially if it is conceived properly and implemented justly and fairly. It behoves us however to note here the often-uneasy relationship, the possible incompatibilities, tensions, conflicts, and contradictions that may exist in fact between these two forms of political and economical organization, respectively democracy and capitalism.[19] Besides, as the cases of China and other so-called 'Asian tiger economies' in recent decades have shown, they are not natural allies or complements of each other: 'capitalism' (or 'a market economy') can be (more or less effectively) combined with a non-democratic and non-liberal system, but rather with a communist, totalitarian or authoritarian regime. Perhaps we will soon come to a realization about the inherent limits

[19] See Schumpeter (1942/1962); Bell (1996); Wood (1995); Street (2000); Samuelson (2005); Charolles (2006) and Reich (2007).

of autocratic development (Pei, 2006). Perhaps we will soon come to a realization of the limits of undemocratic capitalism just as we have already ascertained the limits of undemocratic socialism or 'communism'. But then again, we may instead conclude that such an analysis is itself theoretically limited because motivated by inherently inadequate or outdated assumptions, concepts, and methodologies.

In any case, I object to these systems in themselves as forms and modalities of political and economic organization as we have come to know them in our more recent history. More specifically, I reject the rationalizations typically advanced to 'justify' their merits and advantages without considering possible alternatives which may not be saddled by their shortcomings, deficits and limits as well as their morally objectionable consequences in terms of political, economical, social, cultural, and ecological justice. In the end, such a questioning issues into a call for a *paradigm shift* not only in education, but in (political) philosophy as well.

A fundamental assumption of the approach taken in this essay is that *education* is connected in an intrinsic way with *politics* insofar as the very meaning of education is assumed to be defined by the prevailing meaning of politics (Freire, 1985).[20] In other words, the question of education is always

---

[20] It is perhaps important to distinguish here between two senses of 'politics'. There is 'politics' (as in '*la politique*'), or in the sense of what politicians do, i.e., the games, lies, deceptions, and manipulations they perpetrate on a daily basis in order to advance the interests they presumably represent. In contrast, there is 'the political' (as in '*le politique*'), the incontrovertible domain of the public sphere. In this sense, it has to do with questions of just and fair *recognition* as well as *distribution* which inevitably arise and must unavoidably be addressed by a group of people who choose to live together under certain peaceful terms of cooperation, reciprocity, and moral responsibility for one another, and for the world in which they live. My use of the term 'politics' includes both of these aspects, but it

already political: What (kind of) education? Who decides? How is it decided? According to which modalities? Education for which purposes? And to achieve which of society's goals? Education for whom? Under what conditions? Etc.

Obviously, anyone taking up an endeavour such as the one outlined herein will be confronted with a number of serious and difficult problems: How then should we conceive of 'education', and what should be its ideal *leitmotif*—learning, acquisition-and-accumulation of knowledge, or rational critical thinking, unlearning, and *paideia*? Can education be truly emancipatory, or is it condemned to remain a form of indoctrination or another? Is rational and self-reflective critical thinking itself possible?—especially in view of radical critiques by a number of so-called 'postmodern philosophers' of the very notions of rationality and critical thinking, not to mention truth and objectivity? Can education be truly and effectively emancipatory without a politics of resistance and autonomy (i.e., without regard or allegiance to any forcefully imposed external determinations or authorities)? Can it be such that it aims to give each and all citizens the necessary means and proper conditions for self-determination, self-government, and self-realization, according to their respective conception of the good life as well as for deliberating and participating in

---

recognizes that while the former kind of politics can be changed and even dispended with, the question raised by the latter is inescapable, and characterizes in a fundamental way what it means to be human. In passing, concerning the current debate between Nancy Frazer and Axel Honneth (2003) about the best way to reactivate and update Critical Theory as a theory of social and global justice, I am at this point more inclined to side with Frazer. Not only with regards to their respective conception of 'recognition' but also with regards to the *structure* of their respective theories of social justice.

the decision-making processes concerning the affairs of their respective community.

Finally, what role, if any, can a reconceived education play in this regard in the aftermath of a paradigm shift? It is here assumed that societies can also make dramatic changes through steps of incremental and progressive *evolution* rather than merely through a (long simmering and incubating) *revolution*, i.e., dramatic and brutal overthrow of the established order. If 'education' cannot play such a role, then what else could? Should one hope for a paradigm shift in education only 'after the revolution', so to speak? Or can 'education' play a progressive role under the present state of affairs — as part of what we might call a *transitional politics* of resistance and autonomy — so as to create in the long run the necessary conditions for a more radical transformation of the world, for a 'democracy to come'? What are realistically the chances for bringing about the democracy to come, e.g., a radical or inclusive democracy? Is the 'democracy to come', as Derrida often stressed, always to come, that is, a promise disjoined from any possibility of actual or full actualization? Perhaps, democracy is better seen as an on-going process rather than a product or a given state, for, as Caputo points out: 'there are no democracies, my friends,[21] not yet, for a democracy is still to come' (1997, p. 174). Elsewhere, he also asks quite pertinently: 'Who knows what the democracies are coming to, or what is coming to democracy, or what democracy is to come?' (Caputo, 2003, p. 19).

In the reminder of this essay, I hope to able to give some answers to many (though not all) of the questions raised

---

[21] Caputo is here paraphrasing a quote from Aristotle, 'O my friend, we have no friends', which has also served as a starting point for Derrida's discussion in *The Politics of Friendships* (1997).

here—even if only in an indirect and sketchy manner. For this purpose, I propose to weave a discussion (as I would weave a rope) tied around the following heading: 2. Education, Ideology, Indoctrination, and Rational Critical thinking. 3. Education as *'Educare'* or *'Educere'* vs. Education-as-*Paideia*. 4. Education-as-*Paideia* for a 'Democracy to Come'. 5. Unlearning, Capability, and Governmentality. 6. Transitional Politics: Resistance, Emancipation, and Autonomy. 7. A Parable on Unlearning and *Paideia*: The Allegory of the Cave. And I will conclude by considering briefly 8. The relationship between Unlearning and the Role of 'philosophy'—after the end of Philosophy.

2. Education, Ideology, Indoctrination, and Rational Critical Thinking

In the meantime, I would like to take up briefly the first and perhaps most crucial question regarding the connection between *education* and *rational critical thinking*. My concern here is to determine whether the latter can justifiably be taken as an ideal of the former.

Suppose one adopts 'critical thinking' (and most specifically a rationality and reasons-based conception thereof)[22] as the ideal of education. Suppose further that one characterizes 'critical thinking' as 'the ability and the willingness to decide what to believe and how to behave on the basis of *good reasons*'. Given that critical thinking is thus viewed as the educational ideal, education would then consist in

---

[22]   In contrast, one may adopt instead a *para-logical* conception of critical thinking—for example, one involving creative and bold imaginative leaps outside or beyond the confining strictures of the laws of binary logic and instrumental-cognitive rationality. This is not however the object of my present concern.

becoming more rational. [See Siegel (1988) for example for a defense of such a view.]

Far from being unproblematic, such a claim raises in fact a number of serious questions. Is it rational to be rational? Can rationality justify itself? Can rationality be justified in a non-circular way, without a prior commitment to reason and rationality itself? If not, is the circularity implicated a *virtuous* kind, as opposed to a *vicious* one? Does the radical skeptic's objection to rationality entail the self-justification of rationality by virtue of its performative contradiction? Or does our commitment to rationality rests in the final analysis on some prior (ideological) commitment or (non-rational, though not irrational) *faith* in (the value or power of) reason? These questions clearly bring up the paradox of rationality's rationality.

Such a paradox is of course not new. It is arguably as old as Western philosophy itself, but its solution or dissolution has taken on a greater urgency since the Enlightenment, and even more so, in the aftermath of its radical dialectical critique.[23] Thus, various modern and contemporary phi-

---

[23] Such a radical critique of the Dialectic of the Enlightenment has shown how, following the distinction between 'theoretical or pure reason' and 'practical reason' (as in Kant) the Western world has come to be dominated by an 'instrumental-cognitive reason and rationality' which has relegated to a subordinate role 'practical reason' or 'the reason of ends'. As a result, knowledge and technology are pursued for their own sake, as ends-in-themselves, and we neglect the singularly more important question which consists in always asking 'knowledge for what? For which purposes, goals, or ends?' We have more *knowledge* and *technological power*, enough to put an end to all life on Earth and in our eco-sphere, but clearly not the *wisdom* to know how to use it for our own long-term and sustainable benefits (see Maxwell, 2004 for a very enlightening discussion along these lines).

losophers[24] have defended the following positions, or a judicious combination thereof: (1) Rationality can justify itself; the paradox is apparent and can easily be put aside. (2) Rationality cannot justify itself; the paradox is real and cannot be dismissed or dissolved easily. (3) Rationality cannot be justified in a non-circular way, but the circularity is virtuous and pragmatic in nature. (4) It need not be justified; our commitment to rationality is a historically contingent matter, morally motivated, and/or based on *faith*, albeit one that is both instrumentally and intrinsically significant (Popper, 1966, p. 231).

My purpose in the present context is not to undertake a systematic and fully developed critical evaluation of these different positions or combinations thereof, even though such an endeavour would obviously be desirable and possibly even enlightening.[25] I only wish to sketch out briefly a problematic in order to bring out perspicuously what is at stake, and why it is important, particularly in the area of *education*.

Obviously, the role that critical rationality plays in education is of great import to those of us who object to, and find fault with dogmatic and doctrinaire approaches to the transmission of knowledge and culture, as may be found, for example (but not exclusively) among fundamentalist (religious or secular) groups, traditionalists, authoritarian

---

[24] It would be worthwhile examining and mapping out the specific positions taken in this respect by various philosophers in the history of philosophy, say, from Descartes to Nietzsche, Foucault, Derrida, Rorty, MacIntyre, Popper, Wittgenstein, and Habermas.

[25] Such a problematic has long been of interest to philosophers of education, who are part of the 'critical thinking' and 'critical pedagogy' movements, as well as to critical and radical democracy theorists concerned with the possibility of moral autonomy and emancipation. See Burbules & Berk (1999); see also Endres (1996).

or totalitarian regimes. If there is to be 'a difference that makes a difference' between *education* and *ideology*, between *education* and *indoctrination*, or between *liberal* and *dogmatic -doctrinaire* conceptions of knowledge and cultural trans- mission, then presumably we should be able to articulate an unmitigated defence of the conception suggested above.

Such an educational ideal has naturally been defended over time in various ways, and most notably by philoso- phers drawing upon the legacy of the Enlightenment, vari- ously interpreted. They focused for this purpose on *respect, empowerment, traditions of open and unfettered inquiry,* and *democratic citizenship,* or even all four notions. But, in one way or another, these various defences have had to contend with two serious objections, one raised on the basis of *ratio- nality-as-ideology,* and the other on the basis of *educa- tion-as-indoctrination.*

Let us take 'ideology' as 'a generally distorting and deceptive framework that serves to shape individual and collective consciousness, as well as to guide and legitimate beliefs and actions, and render experience meaningful, and that, furthermore, presents itself all the while as a bearer of "*the* truth" about our reality and our condition in the world as we know it. In many ways, its distinctive mark is that it can never be wrong, and it is right even when it is wrong' (for a definition along this line, see Siegel, 1988, p. 65).

The first objection consists in pointing out that critical thinking cannot be justified independently of any ideologi- cal commitment. The latter is logically prior to a commit- ment to any educational ideal. What counts as a reason depends on what one's ideology recognizes as a reason, the objection stresses. Rationality itself is ideology-dependent. By claiming this, the skeptical objector reminds us of the paradox of rationality, and that short of a solution, the inde- pendence of reason from ideology is surely in doubt. What we need therefore is a justification of rationality that does not itself depend on a prior (ideological) commitment to the value of reason.

Critical rationality does not seem to fare better in response to the second objection from 'indoctrination'. Let us take 'indoctrination' as pertaining to intentions, methods, or content, and as consisting for the most part in the promotion of a 'non-evidential style of belief and belief-formation' (Green, 1972, pp. 25–46; Snook, 1972). A belief is said to be held non-evidentially when it is held without regard to 'evidence' relevant to its rational assessment; it is thus an indoctrinated one. To the extent that indoctrination may be regarded as the cluster of those modes of belief inculcation that promote and foster a non-evidential style of belief, it is clearly anti-critical, whatever else it may be. If indoctrination is more often than not the norm in education, as some contemporary philosophers have forcefully argued (Chokr, 2007b), this would certainly constitute a problem for critical thinking as an educational ideal. Indeed, it is even claimed not only that indoctrination is inevitable generally speaking, but that the non-evidential inculcation of the value of rational critical thinking is inevitable as well.

Suppose we admit that some form of indoctrination is indeed inevitable since all societies inculcate ideas and values in youngsters whose rational capabilities are limited by their stage of development. How could we then go on to defend critical rationality?

We could point out for example that as children grow up intellectually, they would then have the capabilities required to replace the non-rational grounds of their previously inculcated ideas and values with good reasons? We could then say that their ideas and values are somehow 'redeemable by reasons' (Siegel, 1997), and we could even try to draw a distinction between '*indoctrination*' and '*non-*

rational belief inculcation' by claiming that indoctrinated ideas are not redeemable by reasons, whereas inculcated ones are. The problem however arises again when we ask whether critical rationality is itself redeemable by reasons. Besides, there does seem to be a very thin line between 'indoctrinated' and 'inculcated'.

Suppose we have inculcated a young person to accept the assumptions and values of critical thinking. Can we then infer that the plausibility of those assumptions and values are themselves justifiable in such a way that the non-rational grounds upon which she initially based her commitment to rationality could later be replaced by good reasons?

The answer to this question is, as suggested earlier, we can indeed do so *only if* one already accepts the assumptions and values of rationality. Would someone who has truly absorbed and imbibed these assumptions allow such a *vicious circle* in seeking to replace her non-rational grounds for this commitment with good reasons? It is doubtful. In order to shed the non-rational basis of her convictions, she will require instead that any justification be convincing without presupposing that which it endeavours to demonstrate. This is precisely the sort of justification for rationality that is here missing.

Unless we have a viable solution to the paradox of rationality's rationality, there seems to be no basis in the end for the claim that 'critical thinking' is 'redeemable by reasons'. If the very process of reasoning is itself non-redeemable, then there is also no basis to the belief that reasons are capable of redeeming any other commitments a person (child, youngster, or adult) might be inculcated to accept and adopt. The distinction drawn earlier collapses because rationality is not redeemable, and with such a collapse, we are left with the inevitability of indoctrination and the consequent impossibility of critical thinking.

Rather than taking a purely logical or epistemological approach to the problem ('Is it rational to be rational?'), we are arguably better off adopting an ethical perspective ('Why should one be rational?'). Underwriting the various post-Enlightenment attempts to 'justify' critical rationality and stress its significance and importance in education, there seems to be a way of thinking that is plausible at least to those who favour liberal or radical (deliberative and participative) democracy and an open society (see Bohman, 2005). Such a perspective presupposes a 'Copernican revolution' in thought in that it calls for the recognition that we base our commitment to critical rationality on *conceptions of the good life for moral persons* rather than base our conceptions of the good on *rational justifications*. Critical thinking, in other words, is not the educational ideal; it is only a tool that we use in order to achieve such an ideal. Rationality is not the end in view. It is merely a means used to cultivate *moral personhood*. The question here is, as with the case of 'knowledge' previously, 'yes to rationality, but rationality for what ends, purposes or goals?'

3. 'Education' as *Educare* or *Educere* vs. 'Education-as-*Paideia*'

I now propose shifting my discussion to some etymological, terminological, and conceptual clarifications in order to take properly my bearings for the remainder of this essay.

It is interesting to note that there are two different Latin etymological roots for the English term 'education'. They are *'educare'*, which means 'to train' or 'to mold', and *'educere'*, which means 'to lead out' or 'to draw out' (Craft, 1984). While these two meanings are obviously different, they are both represented in the English (as well as French)

word. Thus, as one may surmise, there seems to be an etymological basis for many of the vociferous and contentious
debates about education today. As happens often, the
opposing sides often use the same word to denote very different concepts and meanings. We might characterize this
as the *'essential tension'* of education today. One side uses 'education' to mean the preservation and passing down or
transmission of culture and knowledge and the shaping of
youths in the image of their parents, so to speak. The other
side sees 'education' as preparing a new generation for the
changes that are still to come — readying them to find or create solutions to problems yet unknown. One calls for *filling up*
students' heads with knowledge-content, and subsequently,
for rote memorization, drills, repetition, imitation,[26] and for
turning them in disciplined, normalized and potentially
productive members of the workforce. The other focuses on
producing *well-trained minds* and individuals capable of
questioning, critical thinking, imagination, creativity, and
self-reflective deliberation as engaged citizens.[27]

To complicate matters further, some of the protagonists
expect education to fulfil both functions, but allow only
those conceptions, theories, practices, and activities, which
in the end only serve to promote *'educare'*. For example, the
so-called 'back-to-basics' movement in primary, secondary, and even tertiary education (in the US) has in recent
years gained strength and continues to be very influential
in shaping curricula. The vocal presence of 'the religious
right' has given it the status of being unquestionable.

---

[26] As can be expected, the 'empty-container theory of education' is
typically coupled with a 'mimetic theory of learning'.

[27] I am here putting into play a distinction drawn by Montaigne (*Essais*,
I, 26, p. 149) between *'filled-up or full heads'* (*têtes bien pleines*) and
'well-trained minds' (*têtes bien faites*).

Standardized testing has further institutionalized such a movement as the inviolable principle in deciding what to teach and how to teach it. When teachers' pay and continued employment are dependent on how students perform on standardized tests, teachers will 'teach to the test', in the way they think is most likely to produce satisfactory scores. Teachers most often see memorization and drills on the basics as the most effective way to teach. As a result, the function of the educational system changes from providing a well-rounded, broadly liberal education (which could be of use to future, actively engaged citizens) to preparing them to pass the all-too-important test or exam. Subsequently, what were intended to be minimum standards rapidly become maximum standards, which are furthermore self-defeating in terms of the overall aims of education (as both *educare* and *educere*). In this context, it might be worthwhile exploring the sense in which 'tests and exams' constitute what Foucault might call 'technologies of discipline and normalization' (for details, see Chokr, 2004).

As a result, the purpose of the educational system is not, as common belief has it, to *educere* and enlighten, to produce well-trained minds, and citizens who can act in both their own and their society's best interests,[28] that is, as critically minded and self-reflective citizens in a truly effective democracy. Naturally, the common rhetoric of politicians and educational leaders is that this should be the primary goal of education, but in reality, this is far from being the case. In fact, when viewed from a historical point of view, the purpose of education has been to produce a mass workforce composed of disciplined, normalized, and

---

[28] That is, as individuals whose 'enlightened self-interest' always includes the interests of others as well, in some reasonable way.

potentially productive individuals who do not, and often cannot, think for themselves. Rather, they are more readily prepared and willing to accept without much questioning the directives and orders of the ruling economic, political, and social elites in whose hands power is concentrated and monopolized.

In contrast, according to the Greek etymology, 'education' is best understood as *paideia* (παιδεια) or 'the process of educating man into his true form, the real and genuine human nature' (Jaeger, 1939/1986; Peck, 1962). Because self-government and self-determination was important to the ancient Greeks, its purpose, when combined with an *ethos* (appropriate habits and way of life), is to make man good and capable as a citizen. This education is not about learning a trade or an art, which is called '*banausos*' and is considered unworthy of a citizen, but rather about citizen training for freedom, autonomy, and virtue (*arete*).[29] In other words, it denotes an idea of perfectibility and excellence — though not necessarily one of perfectionism.

In effect, the vision of 'education' underlying this heritage is one that is an integral part of a genuinely democratic society, i.e., a society aiming at both individual and social autonomy — in short, freedom from all forms of undue coercion, external determination, oppression and domination. It is about an all-around civic education that involves a life-long process of learning-and-unlearning as well as character development. It includes the assimilation and

---

[29] Mortimer Adler used the concept of *paideia* in his powerfully articulated criticisms of contemporary Western educational systems and in his subsequent proposals for radical reform (1944; 1977; 1982; 1983; 1984; 1988). Today, a large number of 'private schools' and 'alternative education initiatives' claim for themselves this Greek heritage.

absorption of a broad-based, trans-disciplinary knowledge,[30] as well as the expansion of capabilities that are not
merely subservient and subordinated to the dictates and
requirements of an 'instrumental-cognitive reason', nor to
those of 'economic reason',[31] the economy or the capitalist
marketplace.

Most importantly, it is about the enabling conditions in
the broadest sense for practising a participatory and deliberative kind of active citizenship, that is, a citizenship in
which political activity is not seen as a means to an end, but
as an end-in-itself (Arendt, 1998; Fotopoulos, 1997; 2003).
To be human is to be a social and political animal. The
incontrovertible political question confronting us is always
'how to best reconcile the interests of each and all, of the
ones and the many, in terms both of *recognition* and *distribution*'.[32] Under such a view, one would not only countenance
the feminist motto 'the personal is political', one could even
go as far as saying, 'living itself is always already political'
because it takes place in a human society.

It is here useful to recall the response given by Foucault as
to why he should be interested in politics during his famous

---

[30] See Chokr (2004) for a discussion of the limitations of 'bounded
      knowledge' and the artificiality of 'disciplinary boundaries' as a
      prelude for a defense of 'trans-disciplinary knowledge'.
[31] Whose history is now pretty well-known and mapped out among
      political scientists and philosophers.
[32] *Recognition* of my identity, particularity, or difference — whether it be
      national, cultural, linguistic, or gender-related, and *distribution* of the
      rights, liberties, freedoms and responsibilities, wealth, income,
      resources, services, opportunities, capabilities, or primary goods
      —according to just, equitable, and fair principles of justice which
      provide each and all with the 'social bases for self-respect' and
      'human dignity'. See in this regard, the vigorous and fascinating
      debate between Frazer and Honneth (2003).

debate with Chomsky on 'Human Nature: Justice vs. Power.'

> What blindness, what deafness, what density of ideology would have to weigh me down to prevent me from being interested in what is probably the most crucial subject to our existence, that is to say the society in which we live, the economic relations within which it functions, and the system of power which defines the regular forms and regular permissions and prohibitions of our conduct. *The essence of our life consists, after all, of the political functioning of the society in which we find ourselves* (1974, p. 168; italics added).

The overall aim of 'education' as envisioned here is to develop and expand the capabilities of all members of society so as to enable them to participate in its reflective and deliberative activities. In other words, it is to educate individuals as citizens so that the public sphere could acquire a substantive content, and not be defined merely in procedural terms (Frazer, 1991).[33] This is not to be taken in the context of liberal or social democratic definitions of 'justice', as consisting in the achievement of a certain fairness or the granting of civil and political rights fought for within the present institutional framework of the 'capitalist market' and its presumed natural, political complement, namely 'representative democracy'. Instead, a democratic society under *paideia* would imply freedom from undue coercion and from external determination, freedom from oppression and domination of humans over humans, of humans over nature. This cannot presumably be achieved within the systems mentioned above—characteristic of liberal, statist, or

---

[33] It might be useful in this regard to recall the debate between Rawls and Habermas on the matter of substantive vs. procedural conceptions of the liberal democratic public sphere, and related issues pertaining to their so-called 'family quarrels' as proponents of the liberal democratic ideal (Rawls, 1996, pp. 372–434).

neo-liberal modernity or postmodernity (whichever one prefers), with their inherent concentrations and unequal distributions of economic, social, ecological, and political power. In this sense, it can only be underwritten by a particular conception of 'a democracy to come' — e.g., perhaps, as some contemporary philosophers argue, a form of radical or inclusive democracy.

I would quickly add however that it is very unlikely that a 'direct democracy' could be feasible or even desirable at this stage of our history for all the obvious reasons. More than likely, it would have to take the form of a more effective and real 'representative democracy' in which politics is no longer left to 'professional politicians,' to 'powerful corporate interest-groups or oligarchies', but open widely to all eligible and interested citizens.

In a recent paper titled 'Reason, Representation, and Participation', McBride (2007) argues quite convincingly that the contrast between 'direct' and 'representative' democracy is less important than that between simple majoritarianism and deliberative, i.e., public reason-centred, democracy, as only the latter is sufficiently sensitive to the problem of domination. After exploring a range of arguments in favour of direct democracy, she contends that moves in that direction are warranted only when the practice of public reasoning is sufficiently enhanced. Symbolic representation and delegate democracy are rejected in favour of more substantive measures to formalize communication between voters and representatives as well as permit the formal contestation of political decision on the ground that these will somehow provide stronger defences against domination within the political system. I am inclined to support such a conclusion as well.

4. Education-as-*Paideia* for a 'Democracy to Come'

Clearly, 'education' plays a fundamental role in the formation of 'culture'. I here take 'culture' in a very broad sense, as a more or less integrated, yet complex pattern always evolving and changing by virtue of internal contestations and external challenges (Chokr, 2007a) so as to include all of the major components, elements, or aspects commonly associated with it.

It is also clear that education plays a crucial role in the acculturation and socialization of individuals, i.e., the complex and multi-dimensional process involving and presupposing *material* and *symbolic* conditions of (re)production through which an individual internalizes the core beliefs and values of the 'dominant social system'. Hence, we might say that culture in general, and education in particular plays a crucial role in the determination of individual and collective values.

In fact, we must recognize that, as long as individuals live in a society, they are not just atomic individuals (or 'self-enclosed and self-sufficient monads') but *social* individuals—a point, which has not been sufficiently, if at all, appreciated by some proponents of political liberalism or liberal democracy, and which has often been the butt of many communitarians' objections. As such, they are subject to a process of acculturation and socialization, which induces them to 'internalize' the existing institutional framework and the dominant system of beliefs, ideas, and values corresponding to, and most consistent with it.

To say that the dominant system is 'most consistent' with the existing political, economic, and social institutions does not necessarily imply a kind of Marxist *infrastructure-superstructure* relationship. Both culture and the social paradigm are time- and space-dependent and therefore relative: they refer to a specific type of society at a specific period in time. They both change from place to place and from one period to another, and this makes 'a general theory of history' impossible and untenable, as Foucault's work suggests. I am here alluding to the kind of philosophy of history prized by Hegelians and Marxists in the 19th and early part of the 20th century, and according to which one could determine once and for all the relationship between the cultural, the political and economic elements in society (Best, 1995; Fotopoulos, 2003).

In 'The Structure of the Social', Joseph and Kennedy (2000) provide an interesting attempt to develop a post-Marxist conception of the social structure that rejects forms of economic determinism such as the base-superstructure model and other reconstructions that attribute primacy to productive forces in explaining history and society. It argues in effect that society is the product of complex, often contradictory combinations of many different structures and mechanisms. These form a structural ensemble, hierarchically arranged, but where each element has its own dynamics and emergent powers. It concludes that society is best understood through various conceptions based on *stratification, archeological layering, emergence,* (regular and irregular) *transformation,* and *over-* and *under-determination.* This view seems to me much more compelling.

In light of the social constructivist conception of the individual sketched out above, we could say that people are *not* completely free to create their world as they see fit, because they are conditioned, though not strictly determined, by their history, tradition, and culture. Culture is, in other words, always internally contested and therefore plural (Chokr, 2006a). The acculturation and socialization process is, as a result, sometimes broken. In fact, it is broken in the course of history in almost all time-periods as far as a group or minority of the population is concerned, which refuses to submit to its presumed dictates, or to the one imposed upon it by the majority or the elite. In exceptional historical circumstances, it is so even with respect to the majority itself. In that case, a process is set in motion that usually ends with a radical change of the 'basic (institutional) structure of society' (Rawls) and of the corresponding social paradigm.

Under the view advocated here, societies are not therefore just 'collections of individuals'. They consist instead of 'social individuals', who are both *free* and *un-free*. They are free to create their world — in that they can bring about new institutions and a correspondingly new social paradigm. And yet they are also *un-free* because they are to a large extent created or constituted by their world — in that they have to break with the dominant social paradigm in order to recreate themselves and their world (Chokr, 2007).

In order for a given society to endure and reproduce itself over time, it is necessary that there be some (degree of) consistency between the dominant beliefs, ideas, and values on the one hand, and the existing institutional framework on the other. 'Culture' has a broader scope, and as I pointed out, it is always internally contested; as such, it may express ideas and values that are not necessarily consistent with the dominant institutions and practices (Chokr, 2006a). This has arguably often been the case in the so-called *avant-garde* arts and literature. Examples abound and can easily be found. One could also include philosophy as well, especially when the latter breaks out the 'prison house' of the established canon of the history of Western Philosophy, and deliberately situates itself 'on or beyond the margins' or radically 'against the current' (see for example the works of Foucault, Rorty, Derrida, Deleuze, and Onfray).

In contrast, the dominant social paradigm has to be consistent with the existing institutions for society to endure and reproduce itself. In fact, institutions are reproduced mainly through the internalization of the values consistent with them rather than through the brutal and coercive force or violence of the elites who presumably benefit from them. Obviously, such a possibility cannot be completely discounted. However, the pattern suggested here is borne out and corroborated to a large extent by what history teaches us.

Thus, one could argue that the values for the present dominant system in Western societies, for example, are the ones derived from its basic principles of organization. These are arguably: (1) *the principle of heteronomy* and (2) *the principle of individualism*, which are built into the institutions of 'capitalism' and 'representative democracy'. Such values include the values of competition, aggressiveness, domination, oppression, inequity, inequality, and effective corporate oligarchy or plutocracy—even if its apologists call the system itself 'democracy'.[34]

For the sake of my discussion, I take the principle of *heteronomy* in contrast to that of *autonomy*. By the former, I mean to refer to the fundamental assumptions or premises on which the dominant system is based. These lead to the accentuation of differences and divisions, to the separation

---

[34] This comment applies obviously to the self-declared Western (liberal and social) democracies, but it could easily be extended to the communist-socialist totalitarian regimes of yesteryear and those still enduring today which, ironically, also call themselves 'democratic' republics. In the 20s–30s and for some time thereafter up until 1953 or 1956, the notion of a 'socialist-communist democracy' (as opposed to that of a 'liberal-representative democracy') was still a viable one, and even a real contender for the concept of 'democracy'. However, in the aftermath of 1989 or 1991 (depending on when one chooses to situate the beginning of the end), we must today recognize that this is no longer the case. Only the latter notion, that of a 'representative liberal-social democracy' seems to be viewed as a viable contender at all, and this, despite all the well-known deficits and discontents with such a political system.

of individuals from themselves, from each other, from their community or society, as well as to the separation of humans from nature and their environment and to the control and domination of the former over the latter. They also lead to the creation of social, political, and economic conditions and institutions under which they are 'governed', and in which there are numerous forms of unequal and morally unjustifiable distributions of power, resources, wealth, capabilities, opportunities, and of the social bases of self-respect. These conditions make it difficult or outright impossible for people to resist the established order and to live a life of freedom, autonomy, and choice—i.e., within self-imposed constraints and limits, if any, but with little or no regard for external determinations and authorities.

It must be stressed that what is wrong and objectionable here is not the very fact of the internalization of some values. This is clearly unavoidable. What is objectionable is the internalization of such values that produce and reproduce a heteronomous society, and consequently heteronomous, divided, alienated, and subjugated individuals.

In this regard, it must be increasingly clear that education-as-*paideia* will play a crucial role in the democratic society to come with respect to the internalization of its values, which should be derived similarly from the basic principles of its organization, namely, (1) *the principle of autonomy* and (2) *the principle of community*. These principles should be built arguably into the basic institutional structure of 'a (radical or inclusive) democracy to come'. Such values would include the values of cooperation, solidarity, mutual aid, caring, sharing, equity, fairness, equality, freedom, respect for the person, personality, and capabilities of each citizen, etc.

Would the institutions alone be sufficient, however, to prevent the emergence of informal, but still powerful, dominant, and oppressive 'elites'? It is doubtful. It is here that the crucial role of 'education' arises. The best defense against tyranny or totalitarianism is a truly educated citizenry. I am here alluding to the potentially revolutionary role of 'education', if and when it is conceived properly as an emancipatory endeavour, rather than according to its opposed indoctrination and conditioning function (Freire, 1985). I am not seeking to make a case for Revolution, give new meaning to the term, as some philosophers have suggested we need to do (Foucault in the 70s did so mistakenly, and later retracted his claim; Negri, 2003). Instead, I am interested in arguing in favour of a politics of resistance within the current system, and ultimately for a greater degree of autonomy and freedom for all concerned. I am also contending that in 'a democracy to come', a future, truly and more fully democratic society, education should arguably take the form of *paideia*.

In recent years, a number of philosophers interested in radical democratic politics have upheld such a view.[35] And in view of the mounting discontents with representative democracy, political liberalism and neo-liberalism (Dahl, 1991; Schmitt, 1988; Boorstin, 1974), some even believe that it is today imperative to revisit and revive the *paideia*-conception of education.[36]

Now, it is true that in the aftermath of the collapse of 'the communist bloc', a chorus of triumphalism arose in the West-

---

[35] E.g., Adler (1982; 1983; 1984); Castoriadis (1991; 1997); Fotopoulos (1997; 2003).

[36] It is worth noting that *paideia* was at the centre of political philosophy's concerns in the past, from Plato to Rousseau. However, for some reasons (which are certainly worth exploring further), it seems to have fallen by the wayside in the aftermath of the French revolution (Castoriadis, 1991, p. 162).

ern world hailing the 'end of history' and affirming 'liberal representative democracy' (*cum* capitalism) as simply the incontrovertible and undisputed horizon of our times (Fukuyama, 1992). Insofar as the latter no longer had any external enemies, the 'pundits and intellectual clerks' of our times could no longer imagine our future except as one assigned to us merely by the re-appropriation and further realization of the fundamental principles of the dominant and victorious system. This seemed indeed like a naturally tempting Hegelian conclusion to draw—at least for a while. In more recent times however, even the apologists of such a view have come to accept that democracy's victory is in fact short-lived and illusory. If liberal representative democracy no longer had external enemies, it quickly proved to have many internal enemies. Democracy had in effect become its own enemy and seems nowadays to 'work' (if this is the right word) against itself (Gauchet, 2002; 2007). Its failures, short-comings, and deficits emerged more clearly than ever before, and its promises revealed themselves dubious at best—under the present circumstances.

It is as if, as Chesterton once put it, 'nothing fails like success'. After all, and to cut short a potentially long story, it looks like history is going on—even after the 'end of history'. And that we need not be condemned to the festive dereliction of 'the last men' celebrating their inability and impotence to govern themselves even while they naively believe to have reached finally a comfortable harbour of certainty. We need not be condemned, without hope of recourse, to the motionless frenzy and perpetual agony of the living-dead of post-history. History must go on—because the end is in fact always a new beginning.[37] And the single most pressing question confronting us is therefore this: how are we going 'to make history', or rather, how will we choose 'to inhabit history'?—What is going to be the form of the 'democracy to come'? What kind of 'education' can best help in bringing it about?[38]

5. Unlearning, Capability, and Governmentality

As I pointed out earlier, education is intrinsically political: the very meaning of education is going to be defined in terms of the prevailing conception of 'politics' (politicians' life, political economy or the political) at some point in time.[39] Suppose that we take 'politics' as it is currently conceived for the most part in our societies. Then, it must be related to the present institutional framework of 'capitalism-*cum*-representative democracy'. In this case, 'politics' takes the form of *statecraft* involving the administration of a state by 'elites of professional politicians'. They formulate and set the laws, and claim to represent the people, when in fact they represent the interests of anyone (within the powerful corporate and business lobbies or ideologically motivated political factions and parties) except those of the ordinary people.[40]

---

[37] Should we locate the exact date of that new beginning (or rather, of that missed historical opportunity for a new beginning) on 9/11—as many contemporary observers and pundits who have been 'traumatized' by these historical events are readily willing to do?

[38] It is in such a context that the following question resonates and gathers something like an ominous meaning: 'What (will) tomorrow (be made of)'? [*De quoi demain*...? (Derrida & Roudinesco, 2003)].

[39] As noted earlier, we may have to distinguish different aspects of 'politics'—as in 'politics as usual' or as in 'the political' and always try keep in mind which is implicated in different contexts.

[40] The case is no different in a country like the People's Republic of China, where the people are anything but involved in any meaningful or real way, and where the administration of the State

What we have in such a case is a 'heteronomous society' in which the public sphere is essentially usurped by 'the ruling elites' who monopolize all political and economic power.

It is not surprising therefore that, in such a society, the aims of education are (1) to insure the internalization of the existing institutions and the values consistent with the dominant social paradigm. Each and all disciplines, and even, more significantly and insidiously, the entire system and process of education itself, are enrolled in such a purpose. The values of obedience, docility, and discipline (rather autonomy, self-discipline, and self-government) are central. The second aim of education is (2) to produce 'disciplined, normalized and efficient individuals' who have acquired, accumulated, and stored up enough the requisite 'knowledge, skills, and abilities' (KSAs) deemed necessary to become productive and function competently and efficiently in accordance with society's goals, as laid down by 'the ruling elites' controlling it, and in according with the dictates of 'economic and technocratic reason'.

As Dewey reminds us, however, authoritarian and heteronomous principles in education will never be removed if teachers continue to teach

> certain collections of fixed, immutable subject matter that they were taught which in turn they transmit to students under them. The educational regimen thus consists of authorities at the upper end handing down to the receivers at the lower end what they must accept. *This is not education*

seems to be about anything but the people's interests. It is ironic, generally speaking, to note that countries with the word 'people' in their official name and designation do not involve the people or seem to be much concerned, if at all, with their real interests, except perhaps when the legitimacy of the 'autocratic government' is in question and threatened.

but indoctrination, propaganda. It is a type of 'education' fit
for the foundations of a totalitarian society and, for the
same reasons, fit to subvert, pervert and destroy the foundations of a democratic society (Dewey, 1954; italics
added).

Suppose however that we take 'politics' in another sense, in
accord with a more classical conception, one that relates it to
the institutional framework of a more direct, radical and
inclusive, democracy,[41] then it would take the form of 'citizens' active participation' in which citizens not only question rules, laws, institutions, and practices, but are also
involved in their making. In such a case, we may then talk of
an 'autonomous society', i.e., 'one that not only knows
explicitly that it has created its own laws, but has instituted
itself so as to free its radical (political) imaginary and enable
itself to alter its institutions through collective, self-reflective,
and deliberative activity' (Castoriadis, 1997, p. 132). In
such a society, the public sphere would encompass the
entire citizen body effectively empowered to take all the relevant decisions at all levels. This would have to be the case
not only with respect to the political process, properly
speaking, but also with respect to the economic process as
well, within an institutional framework of just *recognition*
and fair *distribution* of political and economic power among
citizens.

---

[41]   Castoriadis defines 'politics' as the 'lucid activity whose object is the
       institution of an autonomous society and the decisions about
       collective endeavors.' In the same sense, he defines 'democracy' as
       'the regime of collective reflectiveness' (1997, p. 132). We might
       alternatively also characterize it in Sen's words as 'a government by
       discussion' involving each and all citizens. In such a system, the
       criteria for participation in public deliberation as well as the rules
       (procedural terms) according to which the discussion takes place, but
       also the content or subject matter (in more substantive terms) are
       decided by all citizens — as much as this is possible (see Sen, 1999a;
       1999b).

The project of 'an autonomous society' is however meaningless unless it is at the same time the project of bringing forth 'autonomous individuals', and vice versa. It is in such a society that education becomes *paideia*, and in this sense, it would involve (1) civic and political education and (2) capability expansion, human development, and self-creation. In short, it would involve the development of 'the whole person'.

The former (1) would consist essentially in developing and promoting the citizens' own activities as a means for internalizing the democratic institutions and the values that are consistent with them. The aim here is to create informed and responsible individuals who are capable of internalizing both the necessity of rules, laws, institutions, and practices and the possibility of radically putting them into question, i.e., individuals who are capable of interrogation, critical thinking, reflectiveness, and deliberation. This process would presumably start at an early age through the creation of 'educational public spaces' that have nothing to do with present schools and systems of higher education. These will be 'spaces' in which the young are brought up to internalize, and therefore, to accept fully and for good reasons, the democratic institutions and the values implied and upheld by the fundamental principles of organization of society, namely, autonomy and community.

As for the latter (2), it would involve the development of the capability to learn independently, *to learn how to learn*, and eventually, if need be, *to unlearn*, rather than merely being fed or stuffed with useless knowledge-contents, and being able to remember them for the purpose of tests and exams. Only by assuming individuals to be *willful* and *willing* subjects with already 'a mind of their own' can they become increasingly more autonomous, and capable of self-reflective, critical activity and deliberation. As suggested earlier, learning how to learn *independently* cannot really occur unless one is willing and prepared to unlearn in some sense, to a greater or lesser extent. Naturally, this 'unlearning process' presupposes 'learning'; otherwise, it would not make sense. It cannot therefore completely dispense with the necessary imparting of knowledge, skills, and abilities (KSAs) — if only in a provisional way. However, such imparting would now have to assume a different form and be carried out according to different modalities — in a spirit of open discussion and debate, radical questioning, and continuous experimentation.

For one thing, it could make a deliberate and systematic effort to expose and open up students to 'new ways of knowing' (alternative, feminist, and non-Western) and 'new forms of knowledge' (subjugated vs. dominant), critically evaluated and apprehended in their historicity, and in a trans-disciplinary manner beyond 'bounded knowledges' and established 'disciplinary boundaries' (Chokr, 2004). On the other hand, it could take the form of involvement in actual, real-life situations and in the multitude of human activities, as well as guided, critical, and cross-cultural tours of our theories and practices, of our scientific, technical, artistic, literary, and philosophical productions and achievements. The ultimate objective would be to enhance the enabling conditions for learning how to learn, radical questioning, discovering, connecting, unlearning, creating and inventing — and in the process, recreating and re-inventing oneself, if need be. The latter task could well be apprehended according to an *ethics* that is, as suggested by Foucault in his later work, best conceived as *aesthetics of existence* (Foucault, 1988, pp. 49–50; see also Chokr, 2006b; 2007 for a modest proposal as to how we can best make sense and extend Foucault's idea).

Such 'a capabilities-based system of education' would, as Foucault often pointed out, bring home at least one incontrovertible 'truth' about our world, our practices, institutions, and values: *how* they came to be *what* they are is a result of historically contingent developments; they are not therefore necessary, natural or immutable; they could be otherwise, different, and possibly even better. Similarly, it would bring home the incontrovertible 'truth' about ourselves: *how* we came to be *who* or *what* we are, as constituted subjects is due to historically contingent developments; we are not therefore condemned to our fate, to be and remain the same; we could be otherwise, other than what/who and how we presently are. It should by now be clear how this all ties up with the problem of 'governmentality': We do not have to be governed so much and so badly — in this or that way; we can realistically aim and hope for a greater degree of self-government, self-determination, and autonomy.

6. Transitional Politics:
Resistance, Emancipation, and Autonomy

At this point, the crucial question arises: how do we go from the current state of affairs, best characterized as one of '(mis)education' (i.e., based on indoctrination, conditioning, disciplining, normalization, and 'dummification') to 'education-as-*paideia*' (i.e., one that enables resistance, emancipation, self-creation, and autonomy)? In other words, how do we move from a state of affairs in the grips of oligarchic corporate and business interests underwritten and advanced by what I called earlier 'the tyranny of instrumental-cognitive reason' in its latest and most sophisticated expression as 'economic reason' to one anchored in a proper understanding of education-as-*paideia*, and a judicious apprehension of the demands of 'practical reason' whose overriding concern is and remains: how should I/We live?

If one no longer upholds the revolutionary ideal of past centuries and yesteryear in favour of a brutal and violent transformation of society overnight so as to give birth to a 'new (wo)man' and 'a new world order'. If, furthermore, one opposes such a political programme because it seems always already caught up in the grips of a 'totalitarian temptation', then what real or realistic options do we have?

One could opt arguably for a strategy of radical *transitional politics*. This is a politics of resistance that could lead us from today's falsely and insufficiently 'democratic society' based on heteronomy, alienation, narrow-minded individualism, morally unjustifiable economic and political inequalities to a 'democracy to come'. E.g., a more radical and inclusive democracy based on self-government, (individual and social) autonomy, authentic living, community, and a fair distribution of economic-political power as well as self-respect. Such a politics can only be based on some form of *emancipatory education* as 'the missing link'.

The aim of such an 'education' would be to give an answer to the 'riddle of politics' itself (Castoriadis, 1997, p. 131). Such a riddle has to do with figuring out how to produce autonomous human beings (capable of critical and self-reflective activity) within the existing heteronomous society characterized by widespread inequities, inequalities, divisions, conflicts, tensions, separations, and alienations. Beyond that, it has to do with how to deal with the paradoxical situation of educating individuals to accede to autonomy while, or in spite of, teaching them to internalize existing institutions. *It is perhaps most crucially at this very point that one can best understand the necessity and relevance of 'unlearning'.* This is indeed a difficult and challenging situation, but it is unquestionably our predicament at this juncture of history. It would seem that nothing short of a *radical questioning* and *breaking down* of the acculturation and socialization process could open the way for us and create the necessary conditions for unleashing the power of our (political, ethical, and aesthetic) imagination. In short, it would seem that nothing short of *unlearning* (in the sense of *'désapprendre'* pour mieux *'se deprendre'* — literally 'to unlearn in order to better be able to refuse being taken in, and thereby to unshackle ourselves') could enable us to do so.

If emancipatory education is the necessary link between our present state of '(mis)education' to 'education-as-*paideia*', and if it is the central piece of a radical transitional politics from a heteronomous society to an autonomous one, then I submit that *unlearning* must be a crucial component not only of *emancipatory education* but also of *paideia* in the final instance. As such, it constitutes in fact a precondition to 'education-as-*paideia*'. Nothing short of that could enable us to throw off the shackles of the entrenched 'beliefs', 'ideologies' and 'heteronomous practices' of our times, while working together to create and bring about the kinds of institutions and their corresponding values that, once internalized, will enhance our capabilities for becoming autonomous in 'a democracy to come'. In the process, there is no escape from confronting the question of governmentality, namely, how and how much do we want (or not) to be governed, or rather and more to the point, how do want to be self-governed? I take this to be the ideal of a real and effective democracy which remains so far unfulfilled even in the most mature and advanced Western democracies, not to mention elsewhere.

It should be clear from all the above that (1) a politics of resistance and autonomy (implied by a transitional strategy toward a truly democratic society), (2) emancipatory education, and (3) *paideia* are interrelated through the internal dynamics that leads from the first two instances to the latter. It should also be clear that *paideia* is only possible within the framework of 'a democracy to come,' a genuinely radical and inclusive form of democracy—however its specifics and details are conceived of. In such a system, critically-minded and self-reflective citizens composing the entire citizen body would be involved effectively in a deliberative and participative way in making decisions concerning all the affairs of the community. And social justice (just recognition of each and all, and fair distribution of economic and political power and capabilities) would be within our horizon of possibilities and perhaps even within reach, and no longer merely the expression of morally lofty yet empty wishful thinking. An emancipatory education is inconceivable outside a radically democratic movement struggling and fighting to bring about such a society. The entire process does not even get off the ground without 'unlearning' —which, as I have argued, is best viewed as a crucial component of emancipatory education, and a precondition for *paideia* itself.

To clarify the relationships implicated in the view advocated here, I propose to encapsulate and summarize them as follows:[42] No social justice is possible without a 'democracy to come'. No 'democracy to come' can be forthcoming without social justice (Srinivasan, 2007). No 'democracy to

---

[42]   This is obviously a set-up liable to bring on quick and easy objections. Take issue with any one of the claims made, and the whole argument would crumble and collapse. So one might be tempted to think. But perhaps one should think again: isn't there a clear and intuitive sense in which these claims make sense not only when taken one-by-one, but even more so, when compounded together? The argument can surely be beefed up and all the missing premises can be formulated more explicitly and defended more forcefully, but its skeletal formulation above should suffice to convey its plausibility.

come' can be forthcoming without radical and inclusive democracy, i.e., without a properly and substantially deliberative and participative democracy. No radical-inclusive (deliberative and participative) democracy is conceivable without education-as-*paideia*. Since the latter cannot happen overnight, education-as-*paideia* is not possible without emancipatory education—possibly over a long stretch of time. In turn however, there can be no emancipatory education without a politics of resistance and autonomy. We should not forget the intrinsic connection between 'politics' and 'education'.[43] Therefore, no politics of resistance and autonomy is possible or conceivable without 'unlearning'.

'Unlearning' seems therefore to constitute a crucial 'capability', one that is essential if 'education' is to play a transformative and emancipatory role and help bring forth a radically democratic society—or to use Rawls' expression in an ironic sense, a just, fair, and well-ordered society. In such a society, the problem of 'governmentality' would be reduced in the end to the question of 'how we should govern ourselves', rather being governed, in this or that way, to this or that extent, so much or so little, or once again and more accurately with regards to the currently dominant political and economic systems, so badly.

This may sound like a very pessimistic assessment, and unduly so. But I believe the pessimism is justified, because it is more realistic and less idealistic about the current state of affairs. Over and beyond the unquestionable achievements and progress—scientific and social—displayed by the cultures of Modernity and Postmodernity, we must also recognize the profoundly disturbing results and conse-

---

[43] Nor should we forget the multiple connotations of the term 'politics' as it is used herein.

quences that our efforts have led to—grounded as they were in mis-conceptions and mis-directions. The pessimism here at work need not however be the last word. It is justified as a stance only if it issues into a form of radical ethical and political activism within the context of a politics of resistance and autonomy.

7. A Parable on Unlearning and *Paideia*: 'The Allegory of the Cave' Revisited

In order to give a clearer idea of what I mean by the counter-intuitive and paradoxical notion of 'unlearning' in its relation to *paideia*, I would like to revisit Plato's well-known *Allegory of the Cave*[44] in Book VII of *The Republic* (1975; trans. Francis Cornford)—which is arguably one of his wisest and most profound characterizations of the human condition.

I do not do so however in order to endorse the interpretation and conclusions that Plato derives from it, but rather because of what I take to be its significant insight into what characterizes 'education' most fundamentally. For this purpose, I undertake what some might call 'a strong misreading' or 'a deconstructive reading'.[45]

Right from the opening line, Plato states:

---

[44]   According to some cultural critics and philosophers, *The Matrix* (the movie) provides us in some sense with an updated, postmodern version of the Allegory.

[45]   This is arguably the most fruitful way to approach any of the classics of the Western canon in the history of Philosophy. As Deleuze remarked once, the canon of the history of Western philosophy is certainly one of the things we need to unlearn, and free ourselves from, if we are to come up with genuinely creative and insightful interpretations, and eventually create new concepts. In other words, we need to undertake a *counter*-history of Western philosophy, as it has often been advocated by Michel Onfray (2001; 2006).

> Next, said I, here is a parable to illustrate the degrees in which our nature may be enlightened or unenlightened. Behold! Human beings living in an underground den, which has a mouth open towards the light and reaching all along the den; here they have been from their childhood, and have their legs and necks chained so that they cannot move, and can only see before them, being prevented by the chains from turning round their heads. Above and behind them a fire is blazing at a distance, and between the fire and the prisoners there is a raised way; and you will see, if you look, a low wall built along the way, like the screen which marionette players have in front of them, over which they show the puppets (1975, p. 227).

The word Plato uses not only for enlightenment, but also for culture, knowledge, education is *paideia* (παιδεια). He says in effect that the *movement* from 'ignorance' to 'knowledge' traverses a course of *transformations* in the nature of the individual (student). [This may be viewed as a 1st approximation of 'unlearning'.] Education, for Plato, is the gradual and painstaking inquiry requiring that 'the soul ... be *turned around* in relation to everything in front of it' (1975, p. 232). [This may be taken as a 2nd approximation.]

Let's not forget that the cave dwellers are chained by the neck and legs in such a way that they cannot turn their heads, and are therefore unable to move. They can only perceive what is in front of them as they behold the 'shadows' as reality and 'echoes' as truth.

Plato's *paideia* establishes, it seems, an archetype or model in which the constant turning or transformation of human nature must follow on its arduous and circuitous path toward enlightenment. *Paideia* seems to be an overcoming of what was formerly taken to be knowledge (*apaideia*) by a *constant inversion, uprooting,* and *transplanting* of the whole person. This inversion, uprooting, and transplanting [a 3rd possible approximation of 'unlearning'] is possible if everything that is commonly known, taken for granted, and the ways in which it was known came to be different or viewed at least as such.

One may ask why. The answer is that the demand which ordinary given experience makes is an over-powering force of naïve and pre-reflective understanding. This *common everydayness* is considered by the cave dwellers to be the realm, which alone gives measure to all things and all relationships, and provides thus the epistemic and moral ground for directing and organizing the cave dwellers' reality. 'They may have had the practice of honoring and commending one another with prizes for the man who had the keenest eye for the passing shadows and the memory for the order in which they followed or accompanied one another' (1975, p. 230).[46] The silhouettes projected upon the cave wall keep the dwellers' reality under its sway and power. Consequently, the dwellers take this commonplace region of shadows as the free exploration of experience and judgment.

Only a *sudden jolt* can free Plato's cave dwellers. The freed prisoner would be dazzled and pained by *seeing things differently* in the enlightened sphere and would naturally turn back to the shadows for the comfort offered by their familiarity. Though the cave dweller may be less confused with what he previously knew, he is however more *'perplexed'* (1975, p. 229n),[47] and this state of mind may be the index for the onset of a forthcoming painfully acquired understanding and enlightenment. [We have here three

---

[46] This is an obvious reference to the practice of 'testing and examinations' characteristic of an educational system's evaluation and assessment of the students' competences and performances. See earlier discussion to that effect.

[47] Similarly, it is often said that the first torpedo-like effect of Socrates' questioning is to induce something like 'perplexity'.

other approximations (the 4th, 5th, and 6th) for unlearning, what it involves or entails].

As is known, Plato was no friend of democracy, and he interpreted this allegory to lend credence to the authoritarian rationale for his Ideal Republic, which turns out to be 'a totalitarian communist system'. Such a system is far more 'oppressive' than the ones that emerged in the 20th century and that we are familiar with, even if it is led by so-called 'guardians' and an 'enlightened philosopher-king'.[48]

In the end, it is seriously questionable whether education can be viewed merely as an individualistic affair in which 'enlightenment' is possible, irrespective of the broader institutional framework as well as the socio-cultural-political context within which it happens. Such a claim is not only problematic, but serves to underwrite a rather conservative view.

In my view, it should be obvious that *paideia* is not possible outside a genuine (radical or inclusive) democracy. Similarly, an attempt at genuine emancipatory education (including 'unlearning' as a crucial component) is not possible when it is cut off from a effective movement for radical and inclusive democracy, which, as I pointed out earlier, is yet to be actualized in history, and which is best characterized as 'democracy to come' — for lack of a better expression.

Nonetheless, the allegory of the cave dwellers is significant because it shows that education-as-*paideia* cannot be

[48] Some recent scholarship on Plato's *Republic* suggests that perhaps we should not take it literally but ironically, as a cautionary tale, or as an invitation to contemplate the ultimate consequences of a certain line of political thought and vision for organizing society. If such a revisionist interpretation has any merit, it can only uphold my ulterior motive and lend credence to my deliberately strong misreading.

a haphazard affair consisting in filling up and cramming empty heads with all sorts of 'shadows' passed off as 'realities.' In other words, it cannot be achieved, as Paolo Freire would say, according to the 'banking model' of education, or as I prefer to say, according to the 'mimetic theory of learning' or the 'empty-container theory of education'.[49]

Such a theory typically leads to the adoption and implementation of a 'lecturing (or dumping) approach' that involves little or no interaction between teacher and students, and in which little or no participation on the part of the students is expected or encouraged. The teacher acts like an authoritative source and proceeds to 'dump' (from his or her comfortable magisterial standpoint) into the presumed 'empty' heads of the students who passively wait for their daily or weekly rations of 'pre-packaged' knowledge (or what I would rather call cold and watered-down 'soups'). The primary focus seems to be on transmitting a certain amount of seemingly 'structured content' deemed essential, regardless of whether or not the students really understand what they are getting, or can evaluate it in any way.

This approach attests to much of 'the poverty of education today'. It is to say the least based on dubious and objec-

---

[49] Contrary to my expectations, I have recently discovered that Confucius had made a statement to the effect that 'students are not empty containers' (Creel, 1949). This would certainly be consonant with his overall philosophy of education and pedagogical practice: he did not hold structured classes or examinations nor did he discourse and lecture at length on a given subject. Instead, he typically suggested to each student what he should study, and then discussed it with him and sometimes, he reportedly only listened. Often however, he posed questions, cited passages from the Classics, or used apt analogies, and then waited for his students to arrive at the right answer. In the *Analects*, he stated the following: 'I only instruct the eager and enlighten the fervent. If I hold up one corner, and students cannot come back to me with the other three, I do not go on with the lesson' (7.8).

tionable assumptions regarding the teaching and learning process, especially regarding the students' level of involvement as well as their abilities, or rather lack thereof. Furthermore, it assumes that students' minds are empty or do not contain sufficient useful elements already that the teacher can use in smart and creative ways to expand their epistemic and moral horizons, and their already existing capabilities so that they can acquire further or needed knowledge by themselves.

As a result, students are exposed to an incredible amount of pre-packaged and pre-chewed bits and wraps of so-called 'knowledge', which are, for the most part, useless and outdated — not to mention disconnected from the problems and challenges encountered in real life. They subsequently memorize (without truly understanding) a lot of stuff and regurgitate them for the purpose of ill-conceived and ill-implemented tests and exams.[50] More often than not, they quickly forget what they have memorized soon after the tests or exams. For these students, the educational or learning experience becomes a torturous and otherwise boring experience, i.e., a form of punishment.

---

[50] Once again, Confucius is reported to have had the following conversation with one of his students. 'Do you think', he asked, 'that my way of acquiring knowledge is simply to study many things and remember them?' The student said: 'Yes, isn't that the case?' Confucius replied: 'No. I have one principle which I use like a thread upon which to string them all.' Elsewhere, when referring to his own way of learning, he said: 'to hear much, select what is good, and follow it.' He saw 'learning' as process of observation of some type of subject matter whether it be books, objects, or people followed by (critical) reflection that somehow changed the person involved. It is a highly personal and individualized activity charting a middle course between studying and reflecting on what one has learned. Once one is 'awakened' by any kind of real learning, the process is bound to be repeated with joy (Creel, 1949, pp. 135–6).

The desire and joy to learn and know in a genuine sense is more than likely thwarted, rather than sparked off and given a new momentum. The students' heads may be full (at least for a while, and one might ask of what?), but they are not for that matter better educated or better off, with 'a mind of their own', as individual human beings, or as citizens. With Montaigne we should ask: 'Isn't it better to have *'well-trained minds'* rather than *'filled-up or full heads'*?' (*Essais*, I, 26, p. 149).

The reason why 'the dumping approach' is often favoured and adopted by teachers today is because it is more comfortable, less challenging and less risky, and does not really involve special skills, abilities or even much knowledge or expertise — except what the teachers could acquire days, weeks, or months ahead of the students. Almost anybody can become a teacher in this sense. This kind of approach leads many to conclude rather disparagingly that those who choose to become teachers do so because they cannot do anything else.

In contrast and opposition to such an approach, we must instead take care not to alienate students as *willful* and *willing* subjects, and nurture instead those traits and attributes that may contribute to their (individual and collective) interests, their inner life, and desire for self-realization. This would set the stage for a process of thought (theory-as-practice, practice-as-theory)[51] which would supersede *apaideia* (shadows, illusions, and injustice) and open up the way to *paideia*.

---

[51] Indeed, a process of thought that would do away with the traditional distinction between *theory* and *practice* — as a corollary of its previously stated assumptions earlier in this essay.

As I have argued above, education should presumably provide the conditions that permit the individual not only 'to learn how to learn', but most importantly, 'to unlearn', and filter out the presuppositions of cultural silhouettes. It should encourage students to think deeply and critically about the illusory world of all the ideas, notions, and beliefs that hem, jostle, whirl, confuse, and oppress them. For students to perceive their situation as given according to an established and imposed 'consensus' and an unquestioned authority requires of them *a reversal of standpoint*. [This is yet another (the 7th) approximation of unlearning, as I conceive of it.]

An inquiry of this type is intended to help in deciphering the foundations and underlying driving forces of students' thoughts and practices, which from birth generalize and standardize the socio-cultural life-world they are expected to have more or less internalized. In other words, education must consist in moving from *apaideia* (i.e., ignorance, authoritarianism, and injustice) to *paideia* (i.e., enlightenment, autonomy, and democracy). This movement would reveal how the categorical shadows determine an individual's perceptions, conceptions, and even her (cultural) identity. It would also reveal that how a certain discourse or propaganda gathers public and private life-experiences, and makes their content explicit in the name of a credo, which basically says on a note of self-defeating resignation 'this is the way things are (run) around here'. And the silent thought that follows invariably is: 'there is nothing we can do'.

Emancipatory education should also inquire into the origins, sources, or meanings of the socio-cultural-historical context. Its aim should be to bring the questioner into genuine contact with these world contents as they reveal themselves in an *unbiased disclosure*—as much as this is possible through genealogical work [8th approximation]. This process involves the questioner's *dislocation* from socio- cultural forms and a *decoding* of the presuppositions that may obscure their invalidity and lack of merit. [These are the 9th and 10th approximations]. It would reveal that these socio-cultural forms are in fact *ideologies* whose function is to rationalize and legitimize the *status quo*. What constitutes an important element of emancipatory education is a deliberate and critical reflection upon how the student knows what he claim to know, how he forms his judgments, and what kinds of judgments he makes. Interrogation of this kind leads to something other than 'education' for a job placement or employment adhering to instrumental rationalism, economic reason, social psychologism, or mechanistic models that fix self, society, and knowledge into a specter of uniform formulas serving to uphold and underwrite 'capitalism' and 'representative democracy'.

By placing in abeyance the presuppositions and assumptions underlying and governing understanding and behaviour, education, properly conceived and implemented, would thus bring to the fore students' pre-reflective valuations and evaluations. The more students *put out of play* their valuing and evaluating presumptions about the world the more clearly they can view their obdurate effects, and eventually come to articulate a more qualified, personalized and discriminating position. [This may be the 11th approximation of what unlearning entails.] This *conscious-making effort* isolates presuppositions, values, and judgments by requiring if only for a moment the suspension of their validity [12th approximation].

As long as thinking is influenced by the unquestioned descriptions or prescriptions of parents, teachers, bosses, clergy, community and political leaders, self-appointed 'gurus' or 'master thinkers' as part of the consensus-building apparatus for the way things are, students will remain shackled in both their minds and bodies. These protagonists have all in turn and together always offered to think for those who don't think for themselves. Let's keep in mind what this philosopher considers to be sound advice: 'If you don't think for yourself, someone else will surely do it for you' (Chokr, 2004).

Presuppositions always function imperceptibly and often go unnoticed. That is how they functions best. Only when they are *'jarred' from their habitual everydayness* can students begin to glimpse 'the ordering of reality' (or 'the order of things') under which they live. [Here is again another approximation, the 13th.] 'Unlearning' puts into question in a radical manner the validity of all of our presuppositions, which give meaning and weight to 'the established (dis)order of the world', as we know it.

In view of the successive approximations suggested above, it is clear that the notion of 'unlearning' is here stronger and more demanding than what is commonly conveyed by 'critical thinking'.[52] The latter often refers to an evaluative sorting out, or to the ability and willingness to decide what to believe and how to behave on the basis of 'good reasons' that one gives oneself. But obviously 'critical thinking' itself is a critical or crucial component of 'unlearning'. Foucault's expression *'se deprendre'* as a result of 'un-learning' (*'désapprendre'*) is perhaps the best way to characterize what I mean by it. As suggested earlier, this expression implies not only something like the idea of 'not being taken in', but also that of 'unshackling ourselves'

---

[52] The word *kritike* is Greek from the verb *krinein*, which means to discern. Hence, *kritike* (critique or critical thinking) means the art of discerning or the art of critical analysis.

from, of 'breaking the spell' exercised upon us (our embodied minds) by established, prepackaged, or orthodox ways of thinking, being, and doing. It implies furthermore the idea of radically putting them in question in order to more easily put them aside. It implies further the capability to distance ourselves from them in order to be able to seek altogether new, creative and more imaginative 'ways of worldmaking', to use Goodman's expression.

Though, once again, it presupposes 'learning', it radically puts in question its passive and static dimensions of the latter—at least as it has been traditionally conceived over time and across cultures. Instead, it favours a more interactive, dialogical, critical, and historically informed perspective, whose primary concern is always 'the question of ends', i.e., what kind of individuals do we want to become? What kind of society or world do we want to live in?

Ideally, autonomous and self-determined individuals should be able to direct their own education, and become in some sense the 'philosophers of their own education' (Diller, 1998). Only a new social, political, and educational paradigm can help us achieve such a goal.

I submit once again that only a 'democracy to come' under education-as-*paideia*, (e.g., something like a 'radical and inclusive democracy') which seeks a balanced recognition of each and all as well as a more equitable and just distribution of social, economic, political and ecological power, can enable us to achieve it. In the most general terms, it would have to be a form of social organization in which maximum intersubjective experiences are possible, and conjoining to make democratic decisions a reality by questioning the various modalities of mis-recognition and unjustifiable unequal power-distribution. It would be based essentially on the premise that there can be no politi-

cal, social, economic, ecological democracy without reinte-
grating the economy within society, society with the
economy, the polity with nature, and without abolishing all
concentrations of power. It would perhaps give us a way to
escape 'the tyranny of instrumental-cognitive-economic
reason'. It would provide us with an alternative to the current *status quo*, and a way out of the predicament that we
have gotten ourselves in the Modern and Postmodern era.
In any case, it might give us the analytic and critical tools
required for better understanding that our predicament is
arguably exacerbated by the dominant and widespread
belief into the unquestioned redeeming values of
'representative democracy' coupled with 'global capitalism'
— the twin pillars of the so-called 'contemporary consensus'
in this era of the nth wave of globalization.[53]

8. Unlearning and the Role of 'philosophy'
—after the End of Philosophy

In closing, it seems appropriate to consider what could be
the relationship between 'unlearning' and the role of
philosophy — after the end of Philosophy.

I here use the term 'Philosophy' (with a capital P) following Rorty's usage (1979) to denote the Tradition — stretching
from Plato-Aristotle, through Descartes, Kant, Hegel, Marx
and beyond, up to Nietzsche, Heidegger, Wittgenstein,
Dewey, as well as old and new members of the Frankfurt
School (Horkheimer, Adorno, Benjamin, Marcuse, Gorz,

---

[53]   See Chokr (2006a) for a more detailed and historical treatment of my
take on 'globalization'; its novelty, its forms and modalities relative
to different domains, etc.

Habermas)[54]—and its demise as a result of the radical yet judiciously formulated postmodern critiques which have been developed during the second half of the 20th century up to the present.

These critiques have for the most part consisted in radically putting in question many of the traditional aims and pretensions of Philosophy. Philosophy could no longer be viewed as the tribunal of Reason, capable of providing (1) a universalist, ahistorical and foundationalist justification of (the conditions of possibility of) Knowledge, (2) a metaphysical and representationalist theory of Reality and Truth, and ultimately, as the queen of all disciplines sitting in judgment of all other human endeavours. They have also consisted in providing strong and deconstructive misreadings of the classics of Western Philosophy.[55] In short, they provided substantial opportunities for 'unlearning'—in many of the senses articulated and defended herein.

---

[54] Whether or not the last figures listed should be excluded is of course up to debate, but the issue cannot be settled herein. In any case, one must recognize their respective efforts and contributions to overcoming the Tradition. Just as we must acknowledge that several modern philosophers (e.g., Spinoza, Hume, Herder, Schelling, Schiller) were already radically critical of the Tradition and the Enlightenment, somehow ahead of their times, and in some respects 'postmodern' before the term existed. For some relevant discussion however, see Chokr (2007c), in which I articulate my view of the Tradition, as well as evaluate some of the postmodern critiques of the Tradition, as a preliminary to defending the need to reconstruct and renew 'philosophy'—after the end of Philosophy—as a new kind of Critical Theory.

[55] One could argue that every form of philosophizing (Western or Eastern) is, in one way or another, a 'critique' of something. Being critical, therefore, is an attitude common to all philosophical traditions. Indeed, the meaning of philosophy is critique and to be philosophical is to be critical.

However, instead of rejecting any role for philosophy in education or dissolving it into 'witty and learned kibitzing' or 'edifying conversations' (Rorty), or reducing it to just another form of 'textual criticism', 'story telling', or 'literature' (Derrida, Rorty), I would like to suggest a new and more constructive role for it in the 21st century and beyond (for details, see Chokr, 2007c). As I have argued earlier, it must be part of 'education-as-*paideia*' and for a 'democracy to come'. We need to re-conceive and transform philosophy accordingly.

I here submit that Foucault's proposal could be very helpful indeed, i.e., in providing some of the necessary tools (concepts and strategies) for the articulation of a new kind of Critical Theory.[56]

Contrary to the view articulated by James Bohman in this regard, in an otherwise very astute and insightful paper, 'We, Heirs of the Enlightenment: Critical Theory, Democracy, and Social Justice' (2005), I do not think that Foucault's analysis is misleading. It is in fact on the right track, and particularly insightful and instructive about the problem of domination among persons, among other things (as Bohman also notes quite correctly). One may however argue that Foucault is at times too cryptic, and that his project, though on the right track, has remained incomplete, and therefore, requires further articulation and development.

Interestingly, Bohman's goal in his paper is 'to come to terms with the Enlightenment as the horizon of critical social science'. He begins by looking more closely at the

---

[56] One that enables us to move beyond the proposals made by earlier members of the Frankfurt School (Horkheimer, Adorno, Benjamin, Marcuse, Gorz) as well as that of Habermas. For an effort to spell out in greater detail how this could be done, see Chokr (2007c). See also Frazer & Honneth (2003).

understanding of the Enlightenment in Critical Theory, particularly its conception of 'the sociality of reason'. He then proceeds to develop an account of 'freedom' in terms of 'human powers', along the lines advocated by the Capability Approach, by linking freedom to the development of human powers, including the power to interpret and create *norms* (*ethics*), and I might add, the power to interpret and create *forms* as well (*aesthetics*). Finally, he shows some ways in which the social sciences can become 'moral sciences' in the Enlightenment sense. In closing, he claims that such an account provides us with a coherent Enlightenment standard by which to judge institutions and practices (intra and inter-culturally) as promoting (or not) human development, understood in terms of 'capabilities' necessary for freedom.

Here is what Bohman writes in the final analysis about Foucault's project:

> In showing correctly that Kant did not exclude *the possibility of rational despotism*, Foucault argues that there is only one way to avoid the self-defeating dialectic of Enlightenment: *'How can the growth of capabilities be disconnected from the intensification of power relations?'* (2005, pp. 358–9; Foucault, 1984c/1997, p. 317; italics added).

And he goes on to note that Foucault's way of putting the question is on the right track, but misleading insofar as it assumes that a disconnection is possible.

I doubt very much that Foucault thinks of the disconnection here in question in simplistic terms or in the sense implied by Bohman. Let us recall Foucault's view that power and power relations are ubiquitous and pervasive, and that furthermore they do not consist merely of relations of domination, repression, or oppression, but they can also be productive, creative, and even liberating or emancipatory. We would then be in a position to understand that, by putting the question the way he does, he means to highlight and stress what is at stake and the challenge we must then confront. How can the growth of capabilities (i.e., as human powers to do and to be, and as substantial freedoms) be disconnected from the intensification of power-relations (i.e., relations of domination and oppression)? In other words, how can we insure the expansion of capabilities, beyond a certain variable threshold, while at the same time reducing, keeping at bay, or keeping to a minimum relations of domination and oppression, without naturally ever hoping somewhat naively to be able to do away completely with them even in the long stretch of history.

When formulated and qualified this way, it becomes clear that the assumption attributed to Foucault is itself misguided and misleading. For the at times excited, nominalist Foucault, it is fair to say that there is no escape from 'power' or 'power-relations'. However, the always pressing and timely question is always: what kind of 'power' or 'power-relations' are we dealing with? What forms of resistance can and must be deployed in order to gain greater autonomy, open and expand the 'spaces for freedom'?

The essence of 'the political', it would seem, stems from the fact that we can never create an institutional framework that would enable us to dispense completely with 'politics'. We can simply hope to improve the ways in which we do our 'politics'. Perhaps, this is desirable, and not just another ruse of Reason or History — in any case, not a curse.

Bohman also reminds us quite rightly that for Foucault rejecting the Enlightenment *ethos* is not an option (2005, p. 376). He goes on to argue that:

> Contrary to Foucault, the problem of rational domination is not a relationship between two terms, the capabilities of institutions and the relations of dominations among persons, leaving out democracy as a mediating term. A

self-critical Enlightenment puts the problem differently: the increase in capabilities is not self-defeating *so long as the democratic powers of citizens are appropriately institutionalized at the same time.* The problem is then not with increasing institutional powers as such, but with the non-democratic character of certain core modern institutions that are still in need of democratization (2005, p. 359; italics added).

Here again, I find grounds to object to Bohman's reading. It is doubtful that Foucault views the problem of rational domination, as Bohman suggests, merely as a relationship between two terms. To begin with, to the capabilities of institutions, we must add, most importantly, the capabilities of individuals, and highlight the significant fact brought up by Amartya Sen in the articulation of his Capabilities Approach, namely, that the former do not necessarily translate into the latter because of the 'differential or differentiated conversion factors' operating in diverse contexts. Besides, as I already pointed out, apart from the lamentably all-too-pervasive relations of dominations, there are other kinds of relations among persons, more productive, expressive, creative, constructive, and fulfilling relations.

If we grant Foucault a vision of a 'democracy to come' (albeit admittedly it is one that is markedly undefined and unclear), he would, I believe, appropriate for himself the position articulated above by Bohman. Provided however we add immediately that the struggle for the 'democratic powers of citizens' as they come to be enshrined in various institutions and practices is and must remain a permanent one. In other words, it must be continuously reactivated through a process of self-critical reflection and assessment of the powers in question, as well as the practices and institutions in which they come to be embodied or incarnated at different times. As a philosopher of 'freedom as practice', Foucault has insisted on numerous occasions on the necessity to expand and invigorate 'the public reason, critical thinking space' so as to empower people to speak for themselves, to express themselves, to resist, and eventually gain a greater degree of autonomy and self-government. We can safely conclude therefore that he would support a greater and greater degree of democratization across the board within a radical and more inclusive 'democracy to come'.

In his later work, Foucault argued that contemporary society is actually undergoing a 'crisis in governmentality'. People today have become dissatisfied with the various institutions, practices, and procedures which 'ensure the government of some people by others' and which guide people's conduct.

In response to an interviewer's question, 'Do you think the role of philosophy is to warn of the dangers of power?' Foucault responded as follows: 'This has always been an important function of philosophy. In its critical aspect — and I mean critical in a broadest sense — philosophy is that which calls into question domination at every level and in every form in which it exists, whether political, economic, sexual, institutional, or what have you. To a certain extent, this critical function of philosophy derives from the Socratic injunction: 'Take care of yourself,' in other words, 'Make freedom your foundation, through the mastery of yourself'.' (1984b/1997, pp. 300–1).

Let us also recall that in one of his last papers ('What is Enlightenment?' (1984c/1997, pp. 300–19)), Foucault urged us to view philosophy as part of a genealogical-historical, 'critical ontology of ourselves,' whose main question is and remains the question of the Enlightenment as posed by Kant, namely, 'What is going on today?' — or rather, 'What is our present?' How did we come to be what we are today? — and whose *modus operandi* consists in the 'permanent reactivation of the critical attitude'. However, in light of foregoing discussion, I would add that it should consist in the *'permanent reactivation of the critical-and-unlearning attitude'*.

Developments in recent decades, particularly in information and communication technologies (ICTs), have dramatically contributed to the 'rising tide of mediocrity and bullshit' — and to what looks, by all measures and criteria considered, like 'the dumbing down' of the inhabitants of Western societies, and by extension, contamination, or willful exposure, the world at large. Even though some diehard optimists still harbor the utopian vision of (educational and political) emancipation, freedom, and greater democracy that these ICTs may bring about, it is very hard to impugn the negative and destructive role that they have so far played in this regard.

Perhaps history will prove some of them right [Hardt & Negri, (2000); Gorz (2003)] in their belief in the 'revolutionary potential' of the 'non-class non-workers' (i.e., netizens, hackers, crackers, immaterial laborers in the ICT sectors) of 'cognitive capitalism' and the 'knowledge society or economy' in accentuating its already emerging, internal contradictions, and ultimately overcoming or overthrowing it. Their revolutionary or transformative potential, if they prove to have any, will probably be commensurate with their 'unlearning' abilities.

Admittedly, anyone and everyone can now express themselves more freely, but as a result, the world is literally awash in 'a gigantic and noisy maelstrom of mutually neutralizing messages'. Any opinion is as good as any other. In the end, no one is really being heard, or given due thought and consideration. For, as the popular saying goes, 'when everyone talks, no one can be heard'.

In such a world, the 'multitudes' seem rather politically disillusioned, demobilized, or worse yet, disenfranchised. Let us face it: 'representative democracy (liberal or social)-

cum-capitalism' have proven themselves to be inadequate for addressing the problems we face today—nationally, internationally, trans-nationally, or globally. They can no longer carry people's realistic hopes for emancipation, self-government, and autonomy. The arguments of its critics and discontents far outweigh those in its support. In the meantime, the multitudes content themselves with 'a comfortably numbing life of consumerism' in which the satisfaction of endlessly proliferating 'false needs' has become an end in and of itself and a way of life—albeit one based on *ersatz*-substitutes, *virtualities*, or *hyper-realities* ('images' far more 'real' than the 'objects' or 'entities' making up the world).

One can but be tempted to conclude that most people seem to live according the dictates of 'crowd thinking', or what Nietzsche called 'the herd mentality'—except perhaps for those individuals and groups actively involved in various alternative, social and political movements or in alternative projects of self-construction. There seems to be very little original, authentic, creative, critical thinking—if thinking, at all, there is.

Suppose that by 'thinking' one means, as I am inclined to, 'the ability to always say "no" first to whatever one is confronted with, even if one eventually (after a few seconds, minutes, hours or however much later) comes to say "yes" in some respects, to some extent, and for some good reasons of one's own'. Then one must recognize that such a process occurs very rarely, if at all.

Suppose in contrast that by 'thinking', one means, as Foucault suggests, the 'freedom in relation to what one does, the motion by which one detaches oneself from it, establishes it as an object, and reflects on it as a problem' calling for an appropriate 'problematics' and eventually, if possible for a solution (1984a/1997, p. 117). Then again, one must acknowledge that not much of this is going on today.

We seem to have reached a stage in our history in which we are all somehow subjected to a massive, continuous bombardment and assault (for the most part subliminal) of a number of dominant and pervasive *memes*.[57] These have managed, by some historically contingent mechanisms or *dispositifs*, to emerge, reproduce, replicate, proliferate, and 'metastasize' through the whole planetary discourse, our 'collective unconscious', the established *doxa*, *ortho*-doxies, and *ortho*-doxicalities. It is obviously extremely difficult to escape from this bombardment and barrage, which is even more effective and sophisticated because it operates below most individuals' radars, in a stealth-like fashion, and as such, it is almost undetectable to most people. This explains at least in part the global dominance of the *mimetic* and *dumbing* way of 'thinking', learning, acting and living. Not to mention the emergence of a new kind of 'fascism' as "a normative element of culture itself" (Ahmed, 2008, p. 93).[58]

-----

[57] This neologism was originally defined as 'a unit of cultural transmission or imitation' to convey analogically to the 'gene' of biological evolution the self-propagating, self-replicating, and circulating unit of cultural evolution. It is believed that it might prove useful in explaining various recalcitrant aspects of human behavior, cultural development, and evolution. 'Memes' have as their fundamental property 'evolution via selection' in that replication, mutation, survival, and competition influence them. In more casual *parlance*, a 'meme' refers to any piece of information, knowledge, or meaning regardless of its mode or medium of expression that is produced, circulates, is reproduced, and passed from one mind to another. Examples might include thoughts, ideas, theories, practices, habits, songs, dances, rites, rituals, and even moods, etc. There may be here the elements for a fruitful and possibly illuminating inter-disciplinary research program, i.e., that of 'memetics', or should I say, 'mimetics'.

[58] In his recent paper (2008, pp. 79–94) titled 'Mass Mentality, Culture Industry, and Fascism', Saladdin Said Ahmed weaves a very

If there is still any relevance at all to philosophy — after the end of Philosophy, and at this juncture of our history, its task must consist essentially in taking a micro-physical and micro-physiological approach (rather than a meta-physical or speculative approach) to diagnosing all forms and mani-festations of 'mediocrity and bullshit' on all fronts. It must seek to provide opportunities for 'unlearning' by counter-acting their nefarious, noxious, anesthetic, and dormitive, powerful effects across the entire socio-political-cultural-spiritual landscape. Philosophers must therefore be content to assume honorably, as Nietzsche suggested in the *Gay Science*,[59] the role of 'mediocrity-and-bullshit' detector and buster. And since 'charity in good order begins at home', they must turn their detecting and busting capabilities inward, toward themselves and their own discipline, as it is far from being immune to this debilitating and crippling condition.

---

powerful and illuminating discussion based on the analyses of Foucault, Deleuze, and those, most importantly, of Adorno and Horkheimer. See also Chokr (2009), forthcoming.

[59] The ancient philosophers taught that the main source of misfortune was (not 'selfishness' as the 'ascetic' philosophies of denial and renunciation had claimed for thousands of years before, but) something very different: beginning with Socrates, these thinkers never wearied of preaching: 'Your thoughtlessness and stupidity, the way you live according to the rule, your submission to your neighbor's opinion is the reason why you so rarely achieve happiness — we thinkers, as thinkers, are the happiest of all'. Speaking approvingly in these terms of the ancient philosophers who 'deprived stupidity of its good conscience', Nietzsche said that they 'harmed stupidity'. This may well be the most that philosophers can do, and they should perhaps seek to discharge their task and mission honorably. 'The philosopher's task: to harm stupidity' ('La tache du philosophe: nuire a la betise!' — aphorism #328. To harm stupidity).

Postscript

Far from living in a lost or frozen moment, stranded at the end of history, we now stand at a crucial historical cross-road where *what we do, or fail to do,* will decide the fate of all future life on this planet. We would be wise to recognize, as some contemporary philosophers have suggested, that planet Earth has been entrusted to our 'care,' and that, contrary to all the naysayers, it can no longer sustain the plundering, ransacking, and destruction to which we have subjected it for the past two-three hundred years.

Our future lies open before us. However, it behooves us to recognize also that none of the political ideologies — (neo)-conservatism, (neo)-liberalism, (neo)-Marxism, nor any other commonly traded theory — that we have inherited in the 20th century can guide us out of the current impasse in which we now find ourselves.

Neither classical forms of modern social theory nor postmodern social theories have generated the kinds of paradigms needed for developing a radically different alternative to the mechanistic, materialistic, and anthropocentric modern worldviews that deeply inform even so-called 'radical' positions. Recent theories of postmodern science have made progress in this area, but they have failed to develop the critical social theory necessary for ecological visions to have practical relevance or political import.

Social change today demands a radical ecological vision and a politics that heeds the moral imperative of 'ecological reason' and seeks to regenerate nature, so to speak, through the reconstruction of society along ecological lines. It demands an uncompromising ecological politics that challenges the fundamental logic of a globalizing capitalist system based on exploitation profit, growth, accumulation, and the manipulation of needs. It calls for a counter-hegemony in the form of a radical resistance to the dictates of an 'instrumental-cognitive reason,' and in particular, those of the all-pervasive and dominant 'economic reason'.

In this sense, we must therefore continue (some might say, in the spirit of a certain Marx) to envision the end of one kind of history—the one that is organized around hierarchy, exploitation, and alienation—and the beginning of another, based instead on equality and freedom (construed in the relevant space of the 'capabilities'), democracy and individuality (construed in the relevant space of 'governmentality').

The new vision requires however that we become capable of 'unlearning' so as to unleash the creative powers of our imagination—boldly considering alternatives and other ways. Only then would we be able to function effectively as responsible citizens in a reinvigorated political community, and as reflective caretakers and shepherds of the eco-sphere entrusted to us in this corner of the Universe.

History can only advance through the definition of a new relationship of Humans to the Natural World from which they came. This in turn requires a lucid and courageous apprehension of the ethical and aesthetic conditions of possibility of a new way of being (at home) in the world.

References

Adler, M. (1944). *The Revolution in Education*. Chicago: University of Chicago Press.

Adler, M. (1977). *Reforming Education: The Schooling of a People and Their Education Beyond Schooling*. MacMillan Pub.

Adler, M. (1982). *The Paideia Proposal: An Educational Manifesto*. New York: Touchstone.

Adler, M. (1983). *Paideia Problems and Possibilities*. NY: Scribner.

Adler, M. (1984). *The Paideia Program: An Education Syllabus*. New York: MacMillan.

Adler, M. (1988). *Reforming Education: The Opening of the American Mind. New York: MacMillan*.

Ahmed, S. S. (2008). 'Mass Mentality, Culture Industry, and Fascism.' *Kritike* 2 (1), pp. 79–94.

Arendt, H. (1998). *The Human Condition*. University of Chicago Press.

Bell, D. (1996). *The Cultural Contradictions of Capitalism*. New York: Harper Collins.

Best, S. (1995). *The Politics of Historical Vision: Marx, Foucault, Habermas*. New York: Guilford Press.

Bohman, J. (2005). 'We, Heirs of Enlightenment: Critical Theory, Democracy, and Social Justice.' *International Journal of Philosophical Studies* (13/3), pp. 353–77.

Boorstin, D. (1974). *Democracy and Its Discontents: Reflections on Everyday America*. New York: Random House.

Bratich, J. Z. *et al.* (eds.) (2003). *Foucault, Cultural Studies, and Governmentality*. Albany, NY: SUNY Press.

Burbules, N. & Berk, R. (1999). 'Critical Thinking and Critical Pedagogy: Relations, Differences, and Limits.' In Thomas S. Popkewitz and Lynn Fendler (eds.) *Critical Theories in Education*. New York: Routledge.

Burchell, G. *et al.* (eds.) (1991). *The Foucault Effect: Studies in Governmentality*. London: Harvester Wheatsheaf.

Caputo, J. D. (1997). 'A Commentary: Deconstruction in a Nutshell.' In Ed. Caputo, *Deconstruction in a Nutshell: A Conversation with Jacques Derrida*. New York: Fordham University Press.

Caputo, J. D. (2003). 'Without Sovereignty, Without Being: Unconditionality, the Coming God, and Derrida's Democracy to Come.' *Journal for Cultural and Religious Theory* 4/3.

Castoriadis, C. (1991). *Philosophy, Politics, Autonomy.* Oxford University Press.

Castoriadis, C. (1997). *World in Fragments.* Stanford, CA: Stanford University Press.

Charolles, V. (2006). *Le Libéralisme contre le Capitalisme.* Paris : Fayard.

Chen Xiaoxu (2006). 'The Capabilities Approach: Problems and Prospects.' *MA Thesis in Philosophy,* School of Philosophy and Social Development, Shandong University, China. May 15, 2006.

Chokr, N. N. (2002). 'The American vs. The French 'Foucault': On the Analytics of Power.' (Unpublished Manuscript).

Chokr, N. N. (2004). 'What Does it Mean to be Educated Today?' (Unpublished manuscript of a Public Lecture delivered at Shandong University, China, March 26, 2004.

Chokr, N. N. (2004b). 'Foucault on Power and Resistance — Another Take; Toward a Post-postmodern Political Philosophy.' *International Conference on 'Resistance' organized by the Society for European Philosophy,* Greenwich University, London, UK, August 2004.

Chokr, N. N. (2006). 'Even Deeper into 'Bullshit': An Archeological and Genealogical Analysis — In Response to Harry Frankfurt and G. A. Cohen. (Unpublished Manuscript).

Chokr, N. N. (2006a). 'A Fundamental Misconception of 'Culture': Philosophical and Political Implications.' In Botz-Bornstein, Thorsten and Jurgen Hengelbrock (Eds). *Re-ethnicizing the Minds: Cultural Revivals in Contemporary Thought.* Amsterdam, New York: Rodopi, (Chapter 22, pp. 401–35).

Chokr, N. N. (2006b). 'Mapping out a Shift in Contemporary French Philosophy'. *Yeditepe' de Felsefe* 1/5 (August 2006), pp. 86–122.

Chokr, N. N. (2007) 'Forget *Foucault 2.0.*' *InterCulture: An Interdisciplinary Journal* 4/2 (Summer 2007), pp. 1–41.

Chokr, N. N. (2007a). 'Consequences of 'Cultural Complexity'.' *China Media Research* 3(2), April 2007, pp. 62–82.

Chokr, N. N. (2007b). 'On the Paradox of Rationality's Rationality.' *The Reasoner* 1/5, (September 2007).

Chokr, N. N. (2007c). ''Philosophy' — after the End of Philosophy.' Proposal submitted to the *XXII World Congress of Philosophy,* to be held in Seoul, Korea, July–August 2008 on the theme: 'Rethinking Philosophy Today'. Forthcoming book by the same title (2009).

Chokr, N. N. (2007d). 'On Justice in a Globalizing World: In Defense of Cosmopolitan Pluralism.' In K. Boudouris (Ed). *Values and Justice in the Global Era.* Athens, Greece: Iona Verlag Publications, pp. 20–80.

Chokr, N. N. (2007e). « Qui (n') a (pas) peur du relativisme (culturel)? » *Traces – Revue de Sciences Humaines.* No. 12. Paris, France: Ecole Normale.
Superieure, pp. 25–59. http://traces.revues.org/index188.html

Chokr, N. N. (2007f) 'Who Is (Not) Afraid of (Cultural) Relativism?' *Traces – Revue de Sciences Humaines* No. 12, Paris: Ecole Normale Superieure, p.65.http://traces.revues.org/index401.html

Chokr, N. N. (2009). *An Archeology of Mediocrity: A Contribution to the Analysis of the Emergence of a New Form of 'Fascism.'* (Forthcoming).

Cohen, G. A. (2002). 'Deeper into Bullshit.' In Sarah Buss and Lee Overton (Eds.). *Contours of Agency: A Festschrift for Harry Frankfurt.* Cambridge, MA: MIT Press.

Confucius. (1937). *The Analects, or the Conversations of Confucius with His Disciples and Certain Others.* Trans. W. E. Soothill. London: Oxford University Press.

Craft, M. (1984). *Education and Cultural Pluralism.* London: Falmer Press.

Creel, H. G. (1949). *Confucius: The Man and The Master.* New York: John Day Cie.

Dahl, R. (1991). *Democracy and Its Critics.* New Haven, CT: Yale University Press.

Derrida, J. (1994). *Specters of Marx.* New York: Routledge.

Derrida, J. (1997). *The Politics of Friendship.* London: Verso.

Derrida, J. (2005) *Rogues: Two Essays on Reason.* Stanford, CA: Meridian.

Derrida, J. & Roudinesco, E. (2003). *De quoi demain...?* A Dialogue. Paris: Flammarion <Champs>.

Dewey, J. (1916). *Democracy and Education.* New York: MacMillan.

Dewey, J. (1937). *Human Nature and Conduct.* New York: Modern Library.

Dewey, J. (1954). *The Public and Its Problems.* Chicago: The Swallow Press.

Diller, A. (1998). 'Facing the Torpedo Fish: Becoming a Philosopher of One's Own Education.' *Philosophy of Education Society Yearbook,* 1998. Available online at http://www.ed.uiuc.edu/EPS/PES-yearbook/1998/diller.html

Dreyfus, H. & Rabinow, P. (1982). *Michel Foucault: Beyond Structuralism and Hermeneutics.* Chicago: University of Chicago Press.

Endres, B. (1996). 'Habermas and Critical Thinking.' *Philosophy of Education Yearbook,* 1996. Available online at
http://www.ed.uiuc.edu/EPS/PES-Yearbook/ 96_ docs/ endres. html.

Fotopoulos, T. (1997). *Towards an Inclusive Democracy.* London: Cassell / Continuum.

Fotopoulos, T. (2003). 'From (Mis)education to *Paideia.*' *Democracy & Nature* (9/1), pp. 15–50.

Fotopoulos, T. (2005). 'The Multidimensional Crisis and Inclusive Democracy'. *The International Journal of Inclusive Democracy*. Special Issue (August 2005).

Foucault, M. (1974). 'Human Nature: Justice vs. Power'. In Fons Elders (ed.) *Reflexive Water*. London: Souvenir Press.

Foucault, M.(1976/1990). *History of Sexuality*. Vol. 1: *The Will to Know* (1976). New York: Vintage Books, 1990.

Foucault, M.(1979/1986). 'Governmentality.' *Ideology and Consciousness* No. 6, Summer 1986, pp. 5–21.

Foucault, M.(1981). 'Omnes et Singulatim: Toward a Criticism of 'Political Reason''. In *The Tanner Lectures on Human Values. II*. Salt Lake City, UT: University of Utah Press/ Cambridge University Press, pp. 223–54.

Foucault, M. (1982). 'Afterword: The Subject and Power.' In Dreyfus, H. and Rabinow, P. *Michel Foucault: Beyond Structuralism and Hermeneutics*. Chicago: University of Chicago Press.

Foucault, M. (1994). 'What is Critique?' in Paul Rabinow and Nikolas Rose (Eds.). *The Essential Foucault: Selections from the Essential Works 1954-1984*. New York: New Press, pp. 263–78.

Foucault, M. (1997). 'Security, Territory, and Population.' In Paul Rabinow (ed.), *Michel Foucault: Ethics, Subjectivity and Truth*, Vol. I. New York: The New Press, pp. 67–71.

Foucault, M.(1997). 'The Birth of Biopolitics.' In Paul Rabinow (ed.), *Michel Foucault: Ethics, Subjectivity and Truth*, Vol. I. New York: The New Press, pp. 73–9.

Foucault, M.(1984a/1997). 'Polemics, Politics, and Problematizations' In Paul Rabinow (ed.). *Michel Foucault: Ethics, Subjectivity and Truth*, Vol. I. New York: The New Press, 1997, pp. 111–19.

Foucault, M. (1984b/1997). 'The Ethics of the Concern for Self as a Practice of Freedom.' In Paul Rabinow (ed.), *Michel Foucault: Ethics, Subjectivity and Truth*, Vol. I. New York: The New Press, 1997, pp. 281–301.

Foucault, M.(1984c/1997). 'What is Enlightenment?' In Paul Rabinow (ed.), *Michel Foucault: Ethics, Subjectivity and Truth*, Vol. I. New York: The New Press, 1997, pp. 303–19.

Foucault, M. (1988). 'An Aesthetics of Existence: Interview with Alessandro Fontana.' In *Politics, Philosophy, and Culture: Interviews and Other Writings, 1977–1984*. Ed. Lawrence D. Kritzman. New York : Routledge, pp. 49–50.

Foucault, M. (1989). *Résumé des Cours, 1980–1982: Conférences, Essais, et Leçons du Collège de France*. Paris: Julliard.

Foucault, M. (2001). *Dits et Ecrits II, 1976–1988*. Edited by Daniel Defert and Francois Ewald. Paris: Gallimard, pp. 655, 720, 819–821, 1033, 1401, 1547–1548, 1570, 1604.

Foucault, M. (2003). *Society Must be Defended*. Lectures at the College de France, 1975–76. New York: St Martin's Press.

Frankfurt, H. (1988). 'On Bullshit.' In *The Importance of What We Care About*. New York: Cambridge University Press.

Frankfurt, H. (2005). *On Bullshit*. NJ: Princeton University Press

Frazer, N. (1991). 'Rethinking the Public Sphere: A Contribution to the Critique of Actually Existing Democracies.' *Social Text* (25/26), pp. 56–80.

Frazer, N. & Honneth, A. (2003). *Redistribution or Recognition? A Political-Philosophical Exchange*. London: Verso.

Freire, P. (1970). *Pedagogy of the Oppressed*. New York: Continuum Publishing.

Freire, P. (1985). *The Politics of Education: Culture, Power, and Liberation*. Hadley, MA: Bergin Garvey.

Fukuyama, F. (1992). *The End of history and the Last Man*. New York: Free Press.

Gauchet, M. (2002). *La Démocratie Contre Elle-même*. Paris: Gallimard.

Gauchet, M. (2007). *L'Avènement de la Démocratie*. Vol. 1 : *La Revolution Moderne*. Vol. 2: *La Crise du Libéralisme* 1880–1914. Paris: Gallimard.

Gordon, C. (1980). *Power/Knowledge: Selected Interviews and Other Writings, 1972–1977 by Michel Foucault*. New York: Random House.

Gorz, A. (1983). *Les Chemins du Paradis*. Paris : Galilée

Gorz, A. (1991). *Capitalisme, Socialisme, Ecologie*. Paris: Galilée.

Gorz, A. (1997). *Misère du Présent, Richesse du Possible*. Paris: Galilée.

Gorz, A. (2003). *L'Immatériel*. Paris: Galilée.

Green, T. (1972). 'Indoctrination and Belief.' In I. A. Snook (ed.), *Concepts of Indoctrination*. London: Routledge and Kegan Paul.

Hardt, M. & Negri, A. (2000). *Empire*. Cambridge, MAL Harvard University Press.

Hekman, S. (1996). 'Radical Plural Democracy: A New Theory for the Left?' *Negations* (96), 1–21.

Jaeger, W. (1939/1986). *Paideia: The Ideals of Greek Culture*. 3 vol. Trans. Gilbert Highet. Oxford: Oxford University Press.

Joseph, J. & Kennedy, S. (2000). 'The Structure of the Social.' *Philosophy of the Social Sciences* (30/4), 508–527.

Laclau, E. (1988). 'Politics and the Limits of Modernity.' In Andrew Ross (ed.), *Universal Abandon?*. Minneapolis: University of Minnesota Press, pp. 63–82.

Laclau, E. & Mouffe, C. (1985). *Hegemony and Socialist Strategy: Towards a Radical Democratic Politics*. Trans. Moore & Cammack. London: Verso.

Maxwell, N. (2004). *From Knowledge to Wisdom: A Revolution for Science and the Humanities*. London: Pentire Press.

McBride, C. (2007). 'Reason, Representation, and Participation.' *Res Publica*. (13/4), December 2007.

Montaigne. (1962). *Œuvres Complètes : Les Essais I* [1580]. Paris: Gallimard, Collection La Pleiade.

Mouffe, C. (1988). 'Radical Democracy: Modern or Postmodern?' In Andrew Ross (ed.), *Universal Abandon?* Minneapolis: University of Minnesota Press, pp. 31–45.

Mouffe, C. (1990) 'Radical Democracy or Liberal Democracy?' *Socialist Review* (20/2), pp. 57–66.

Mouffe, C. (ed.) (1992a). 'Democratic Politics Today.' In *Dimensions of Radical Democracy*. New York: Verso, pp. 1–14.

Mouffe, C. (1992b). *The Return of the Political*. NY: Routledge.

Mouffe, C. (2000). *The Democratic Paradox*. London: Verso.

Mummery, J. (2005). 'Rethinking the Democratic Project: Rorty, Mouffe, Derrida and Democracy to Come.' *Borderlands*, e-Journal (4/1), pp. 1–9.

Negri, A. (2003). *Time for Revolution*. NY: Continuum Books.

Nietzsche, F. (1974). *The Gay Science*. New York: Vintage Books.

Nussbaum, M. (1988). 'Nature, Function, and Capability.' *Oxford Studies in Ancient Philosophy*, Suppl. Vol. 1, pp. 145–84.

Nussbaum, M. (1992). 'Human Functioning and Social Justice: In Defense of Aristotelian Essentialism'. *Political Theory* (20), pp. 202–46.

Nussbaum, M. (1993). 'Non-Relative Virtues: An Aristotelian Approach'. In Martha Nussbaum and Amartya Sen (Eds.) *The Quality of Life*. Oxford: Clarendon Press, pp. 242–69.

Nussbaum, M. (2000a). *Women and Human Development: The Capabilities Approach*. Cambridge: Cambridge University Press.

Nussbaum, M. (2000b). 'Aristotle, Politics, and Human Capabilities: A Response to Anthony, Arneson, Charlesworth, and Mulgan.' *Ethics* (111), pp. 102–40.

Nussbaum, M. (2003) 'Capabilities as Fundamental Entitlements: Sen and Social Justice.' *Feminist Economics* 9 (July/Nov.), pp. 33–59.

Nussbaum, M. (2006). 'Education and Democratic Citizenship: Capabilities and Quality Education.' *Journal of Human Development* 7 (3), 385–95. See also her Lecture 'Education for Democratic Citizenship' delivered on the occasion of the awarding of degree of Doctor Honoris Causa at the Institute of Social Studies, The Hague, The Netherlands, March 9, 2006.

O'Farrell, C. (2005). *Michel Foucault*. London : Sage Publications.

Onfray, M. (2001). *Anti-manuel de Philosophie*. Rosny, France: Editions Bréal.

Onfray, M. (2006). *Contre-Histoire de la Philosophie*. Vol. I & II. Paris: Grasset.

Peck, H. T. (1962). *Harpers Dictionary of Classical Literature and Antiquities*. New York: Cooper Square Pub.

Pei, M. (2006). *China's Trapped Transition: The Limits of Developmental Autocracy*. MA: Harvard University Press.

Plato. (1975). *The Republic*. Trans. Francis Cornford. New York: Oxford University Press.

Popper, K. (1966). *The Open Society and Its Enemies*. Princeton, NJ: Princeton University Press.

Puolimatka, T. (1995). *Democracy and Education: The Critical Citizen as an Educational Aim*. Helsinki: The Finnish Academy of Science and Letters.

Rabinow, P. (1997). *Michel Foucault: Ethics, Subjectivity and Truth*, Vol. I. New York: The New Press.

Rabinow, P. & Rose, N. (1997). *The Essential Foucault. Selections from Essential Works of Foucault 1954-1984*. New York: The New Press.

Rawls, J. (1996). *Political Liberalism*. New York: Columbia University Press.

Reich, R. B. (2007). 'How Capitalism is Killing Democracy.' Foreign Affairs, September/October 2007.

Rorty, R. (1979). *Philosophy and the Mirror of Nature*. Princeton, NJ: Princeton University Press.

Rorty, R. (1983). 'Postmodern Bourgeois Liberalism.' *Journal of Philosophy*, (80).

Rorty, R. (1989). *Contingency, Irony, and Solidarity*. Cambridge University Press.

Rorty, R. (1991). *Objectivity, Relativism, and Truth*. Cambridge University Press.

Rorty, R. (1998a). *Achieving Our Country: Leftist Thought in Twentieth Century America*. Cambridge, MA: Harvard University Press.

Rorty, R. (1998b). *Truth and Progress*. Cambridge: Cambridge University Press.

Rorty, R. (1999). *Philosophy and Social Hope*. New York: Penguin Books.

Samuelson, R. J. (2005). 'Capitalism vs. Democracy.' *Newsweek*, October 3.

Schmitt, C. (1988). *Crisis of Parliamentary Democracy*. MIT Press.

Schumpeter, J. (1962). *Capitalism, Socialism, and Democracy*. (First published in 1942). New York: Harper Perennial.

Sen, A. (1984). *Resources, Values, and Development*. Cambridge, MA: Harvard University Press, Parts IV and V.

Sen, A. (1985). 'Well-Being, Agency, and Freedom: The Dewey Lectures, 1984.' *Journal of Philosophy*, (82).

Sen, A. (1987). *The Standard of Living*. Cambridge University Press, pp. 1–38.

Sen, A. (1992). 'Functionings and Capability.' In *Inequality Re-Examined*. Cambridge, MA: Harvard University Press, chapter 3.

Sen, A. (1993). 'Capability and Well-Being.' In Martha Nussbaum and Amartya Sen (eds.), *The Quality of Life*. Oxford: Clarendon Press, pp. 30–53.

Sen, A. (1999a). 'Democracy as a Universal Value.' *Journal of Democracy* (10/3).

Sen, A. (1999b). 'The Importance of Democracy.' In *Development as Freedom*, New York: Anchor Books, pp. 149–59.

Siegel, H. (1988). *Educating Reason: Rationality, Critical Thinking, and Education*. New York: Routledge.

Siegel, H. (1997). *Rationality Redeemed: Further Dialogue on an Educational Ideal*. New York: Routledge.

Smart, B. (1992). 'Review of the Foucault Effect.' *Sociology* (26/3), pp. 559–60.

Snook, I. A. (ed.). (1972). *Concepts of Indoctrination*. London: Routledge & Kegan Paul.

Srinivasan, S. (2007). 'No Democracy without Justice: Political Freedom in Amartya Sen's Capability Approach'. *Journal of Human Development* (8/3) (November 2007), pp. 457–80.

Street, P. (2000). 'Capitalism and Democracy 'Don't Mix Very Well''. *Zmag.org*, February 2000.

Tarrant, J. M. (1989). *Democracy and Education*. New York: Ashgate Publishing.

Wood, E. M. (1995). *Democracy against Capitalism: Renewing Historical Materialism*. Cambridge University Press.

Index

2008–2009

SOCIETAS

essays in political and cultural criticism
imprint-academic.com/societas

Who Holds the Moral High Ground?

Colin J Beckley and Elspeth Waters

Meta-ethical attempts to define concepts such as 'goodness', 'right and wrong', 'ought' and 'ought not', have proved largely futile, even over-ambitious. Morality, it is argued, should therefore be directed primarily at the reduction of suffering, principally because the latter is more easily recognisable and accords with an objective view and requirements of the human condition. All traditional and contemporary perspectives are without suitable criteria for evaluating moral dilemmas and without such guidance we face the potent threat of sliding to a destructive moral nihilism. This book presents a possible set of defining characteristics for the foundation of moral evaluations, taking into consideration that the female gender may be better disposed to ethical leadership.

128 pp., £8.95/$17.90, 9781845401030 (pbk.), January 2008, *Societas,* Vol.32

Froude Today

John Coleman

A.L. Rowse called fellow-historian James Anthony Froude the 'last great Victorian awaiting revival'. The question of power is the problem that perplexes every age: in his historical works Froude examined how it applied to the Tudor period, and defended Carlyle against the charge that he held the doctrine that 'Might is Right'.

Froude applied his analysis of power to the political classes of his own time and that is why his writings are just as relevant today. The historian and the prophet look into the inner meaning of events – and that is precisely what Froude did – and so are able to make judgments which apply to ages far beyond their own. The last chapters imagine what Froude would have said had he been here today.

96 pp., £8.95/$17.90, 9781845401047 (pbk.), March 2008, *Societas,* Vol.33

The Enemies of Progress

Austin Williams

This polemical book examines the concept of sustainability and presents a critical exploration of its all-pervasive influence on society, arguing that sustainability, manifested in several guises, represents a pernicious and corrosive doctrine that has survived primarily because there seems to be no alternative to its canon: in effect, its bi-partisan appeal has depressed critical engagement and neutered politics.

It is a malign philosophy of misanthropy, low aspirations and restraint. This book argues for a destruction of the mantra of sustainability, removing its unthinking status as orthodoxy, and for the reinstatement of the notions of development, progress, experimentation and ambition in its place.

Al Gore insists that the 'debate is over'. Here the auhtor retorts that it is imperative to argue against the moralizing of politics.

Austin Williams tutors at the Royal College of Art and Bartlett School of Architecture.

96 pp., £8.95/$17.90, 9781845400989 (pbk.), May 2008, *Societas,* Vol.34

Forgiveness: How Religion Endangers Morality

R.A. Sharpe

In his book *The Moral Case against Religious Belief* (1997), the author argued that some important virtues cease to be virtues at all when set in a religious context, and that, consequently, a religious life is, in many respects, not a good life to lead. In this sequel, his tone is less generous to believers than hitherto, because 'the intervening decade has brought home to us the terrible results of religious conviction'.

R.A. Sharpe was Professor Emeritus at St David's College, Lampeter. The manuscript of *Forgiveness* was prepared for publication by his widow, the philosopher Lynne Sharpe.

128 pp., £8.95 / $17.90, 9781845400835 (pbk.), July 2008, (*Societas* edition), Vol.35

To qualify for the reduced (subscription) price of £5/$10 for current and future volumes (£2.50/$5.00 for back volumes), please use the enclosed direct debit form or order via imprint-academic.com/societas

Healing, Hype or Harm? Scientists Investigate Complementary or Alternative Medicine

Edzard Ernst (ed.)

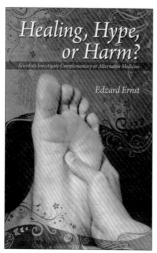

The scientists writing this book are not 'against' complementary or alternative medicine (CAM), but they are very much 'for' evidence-based medicine and single standards. They aim to counter-balance the many uncritical books on CAM and to stimulate intelligent, well-informed public debate.

TOPICS INCLUDE: What is CAM? Why is it so popular? Patient choice; Reclaiming compassion; Teaching CAM at university; Research on CAM; CAM in court; Ethics and CAM; Politics and CAM; Homeopathy in context; Concepts of holism in medicine; Placebo, deceit and CAM; Healing but not curing; CAM and the media.

Edzard Ernst is Professor of Complementary Medicine, Universities of Exeter and Plymouth.

190 pp., £8.95/$17.90, 9781845401184 (pbk.), Sept. 2008, *Societas,* Vol.36

The Balancing Act: National Identity and Sovereignty for Britain in Europe

Atsuko Ichijo

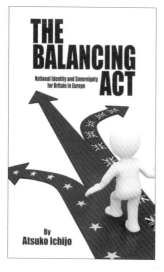

This is a careful examination of the historical formation of Britain and of key moments in its relations with the European powers. The author looks at the governing discourses of politicians, the mass media, and the British people.

The rhetoric of sovereignty among political elites and the population at large is found to conceive of Britain's engagement with Europe as a zero-sum game. A second theme is the power of geographical images – island Britain – in feeding the idea of the British nation as by nature separate and autonomous. It follows that the EU is seen as 'other' and involvement in European decision-making tends to be viewed in terms of threat. This is naive, as nation-states are not autonomous, economically, militarily or politically. Only pooling sovereignty can maximize their national interests.

Atsuko Ichijo is Senior Researcher in European Studies at Kingston University.

150 pp., £8.95/$17.90, 9781845401153 (pbk.), Nov. 2008, *Societas,* Vol.37

Seeking Meaning and Making Sense

John Haldane

Here is an engaging collection of short essays that range across philosophy, politics, general culture, morality, science, religion and art.

The author contributes regularly to *The Scotsman* and a number of radio programmes. Many of these essays began life in this way, and retain their direct fresh style.

The focus is on questions of Meaning, Value and Understanding. Topics include: Making sense of religion, Making sense of society, Making sense of evil, Making sense of art and science, Making sense of nature.

John Haldane is Professor of Philosophy and Director of the Centre for Ethics, Philosophy and Public Affairs in the University of St Andrews.

128 pp., £8.95/$17.90, 9781845401221 (pbk.), Jan. 2009, *Societas,* Vol.38

Independent: The Rise of the Non-aligned Politician

Richard Berry

Martin Bell, Ken Livingstone and Richard Taylor (the doctor who became an MP to save his local hospital) are the best known of a growing band of British politicians making their mark outside the traditional party system.

Some (like Livingstone) have emerged from within the old political system that let them down, others (Bell, Taylor) have come into politics from outside in response to a crisis of some kind, often in defence of a perceived threat to their local town or district.

Richard Berry traces this development by case studies and interviews to test the theory that these are not isolated cases, but part of a permanent trend in British politics, a shift away from the party system in favour of independent non-aligned representatives of the people.

Richard Berry is a political and policy researcher and writer.

128 pp., £8.95/$17.90, 9781845401283 (pbk.), March 2009, *Societas,* Vol.39

2009

Progressive Secular Society and other essays relevant to secularism

Tom Rubens

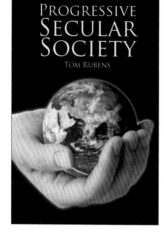

A progressive secular society is one committed to the widening of scientific knowledge and humane feeling. It regards humanity as part of physical nature and opposes any appeal to supernatural agencies or explanations. In particular, human moral perspectives are human creations and the only basis for ethics.

Secular values need re-affirming in the face of the resurgence of aggressive supernatural religious doctrines and practices. This book gives a set of 'secular thoughts for the day' – many only a page or two long – on topics as varied as Shakespeare and Comte, economics, science and social action.

Tom Rubens teaches in the humanities at secondary and tertiary levels.

128 pp., £8.95/$17.90, 9781845401320 (pbk.), May 2009, *Societas,* Vol.40

Self and Society (enlarged second edition)

William Irwin Thompson

The book contains a series of essays on the evolution of culture, dealing with topics including the city and consciousness, evolution of the afterlife, literary and mathematical archetypes, machine consciousness and the implications of 9/11 and the invasion of Iraq for the development of planetary culture.

This enlarged edition contains an additional new second part, added to include chapters on 'Natural Drift and the Evolution of Culture' and 'The Transition from Nation-State to Noetic Polity' as well as two shorter reflective pieces.

The author is a poet, cultural historian and founder of the Lindisfarne Association. His many books include *Coming into Being: Artifacts and Texts in the Evolution of Consciousness*.

150 pp., £8.95/$17.90, 9781845401337 (pbk.), July 2009, *Societas,* Vol.41

Universities: The Recovery of an Idea (revised second edition)
Gordon Graham

RAE, teaching quality assessment, student course evaluation, modularization – these are all names of innovations in modern British universities. How far do they constitute a significant departure from traditional academic concerns? Using themes from J.H.Newman's *The Idea of a University* as a starting point, this book aims to address these questions.

'It is extraordinary how much Graham has managed to say (and so well) in a short book.' **Alasdair MacIntyre**

£8.95/$17.90, 9781845401276 (pbk), *Societas* V.1

God in Us: A Case for Christian Humanism
Anthony Freeman

God In Us is a radical representation of the Christian faith for the 21st century. Following the example of the Old Testament prophets and the first-century Christians it overturns received ideas about God. God is not an invisible person 'out there' somewhere, but lives in the human heart and mind as 'the sum of all our values and ideals' guiding and inspiring our lives.

The Revd. Anthony Freeman was dismissed from his parish for publishing this book, but remains a priest in the Church of England.

'Brilliantly lucid.' *Philosophy Now*
'A brave and very well-written book' *The Freethinker*

£8.95/$17.90, 9780907845171 (pbk), *Societas* V.2

The Case Against the Democratic State
Gordon Graham

This essay contends that the gross imbalance of power in the modern state is in need of justification and that democracy simply masks this need with the illusion of popular sovereignty. The book points out the emptiness of slogans like 'power to the people', as individual votes do not affect the outcome of elections, but concludes that democracy can contribute to civic education.

'Challenges the reigning orthodoxy'. *Mises Review*

'Political philosophy in the best analytic tradition… scholarly, clear, and it does not require a professional philosopher to understand it' *Philosophy Now*

'An excellent candidate for inclusion on an undergraduate syllabus.' *Independent Review*

£8.95/$17.90, 9780907845386 (pbk), *Societas* V.3

The Last Prime Minister

Graham Allen MP

This book shows how Britain has acquired an executive presidency by stealth. It is the first ever attempt to codify the Prime Minister's powers, many hidden in the mysteries of the royal prerogative. This timely second edition takes in new issues, including Parliament's impotence over Iraq.

'Iconoclastic, stimulating and well-argued.' **Vernon Bogdanor**, *Times Higher Education Supplement*

'Well-informed and truly alarming.' **Peter Hennessy**

'Should be read by anybody interested in the constitution.' **Anthony King**

£8.95/$17.90, 9780907845416 (pbk), *Societas* V.4

The Liberty Option

Tibor R. Machan

The Liberty Option advances the idea that it is the society organised on classical liberal principles that serves justice best, leads to prosperity and encourages the greatest measure of individual virtue. The book contrasts this Lockean ideal with the various statist alternatives, defends it against its communitarian critics and lays out some of its more significant policy implications. The author teaches ethics at Chapman University. His books on classical liberal theory include *Classical Individualism* (Routledge, 1998).

£8.95/$17.90, 9780907845638 (pbk), *Societas* V.5

Democracy, Fascism & the New World Order

Ivo Mosley

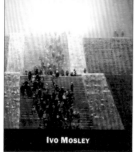

Growing up as the grandson of Sir Oswald, the 1930s blackshirt leader, made Ivo Mosley consider fascism with a deep and acutely personal interest. Whereas conventional wisdom sets up democracy and fascism as opposites, to ancient political theorists democracy had an innate tendency to lead to extreme populist government, and provided unscrupulous demagogues with the ideal opportunity to seize power. In *Democracy, Fascism and the New World Order* Mosley argues that totalitarian regimes may well be the logical outcome of unfettered mass democracy.

'Brings a passionate reasoning to the analysis'. *Daily Mail*

'Read Mosley's, in many ways, excellent book. But read it critically.' **Edward Ingram**, *Philosophy Now*

£8.95/$17.90, 9780907845645 (pbk), *Societas* V.6

Off With Their Wigs!

Charles Banner and Alexander Deane

On June 12, 2003, a press release concerning a Cabinet reshuffle declared as a footnote that the ancient office of Lord Chancellor was to be abolished and that a new supreme court would replace the House of Lords as the highest appeal court. This book critically analyses the Government's proposals and looks at the various alternative models for appointing judges and for a new court of final appeal.

'A cogently argued critique.' *Commonwealth Lawyer*

£8.95/$17.90, 9780907845843 (pbk), *Societas* V.7

The Modernisation Imperative

Bruce Charlton & Peter Andras

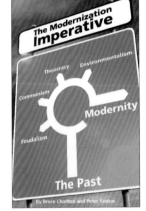

Modernisation gets a bad press in the UK, and is blamed for increasing materialism, moral fragmentation, the dumbing-down of public life, declining educational standards, occupational insecurity and rampant managerialism. But modernisation is preferable to the likely alternative of lapsing back towards a 'medieval' world of static, hierarchical and coercive societies – the many and serious criticisms of modernisation should be seen as specific problems relating to a process that is broadly beneficial for most of the people, most of the time.

'A powerful and new analysis'. **Matt Ridley**

£8.95/$17.90, 9780907845522 (pbk), *Societas* V.8

Self and Society, *William Irwin Thompson*

£8.95/$17.90, 9780907845829 (pbk), *Societas* V.9
now superceded by Vol.41 (see above, p.S6)

The Party's Over

Keith Sutherland

This book questions the role of the party in the post-ideological age and concludes that government ministers should be appointed by headhunters and held to account by a parliament selected by lot.

'Sutherland's model of citizen's juries ought to have much greater appeal to progressive Britain.' *Observer*

'An extremely valuable contribution.' *Tribune*

'A political essay in the best tradition – shrewd, erudite, polemical, partisan, mischievous and highly topical.' *Contemporary Political Theory*

£8.95/$17.90, 9780907845515 (pbk), *Societas* V.10

Our Last Great Illusion

Rob Weatherill

This book aims to refute, primarily through the prism of modern psychoanalysis and postmodern theory, the notion of a return to nature, to holism, or to a pre-Cartesian ideal of harmony and integration. Far from helping people, therapy culture's utopian solutions may be a cynical distraction, creating delusions of hope. Yet solutions proliferate in the free market; this is why therapy is our last great illusion. The author is a psychoanalytic psychotherapist and lecturer, Trinity College, Dublin.

'Challenging, but well worth the engagement.' *Network*

£8.95/$17.90, 9780907845959 (pbk), *Societas* V.11

The Snake that Swallowed its Tail

Mark Garnett

Liberal values are the hallmark of a civilised society, but depend on an optimistic view of the human condition, Stripped of this essential ingredient, liberalism has become a hollow abstraction. Tracing its effects through the media, politics and the public services, the book argues that hollowed-out liberalism has helped to produce our present discontent.

'This arresting account will be read with profit by anyone interested in the role of ideas in politics.'
John Gray, *New Statesman*

'A spirited polemic addressing the malaise of British politics.' **Michael Freeden**, *The European Legacy*

£8.95/$17.90, 9780907845881 (pbk), *Societas* V.12

Why the Mind is Not a Computer

Raymond Tallis

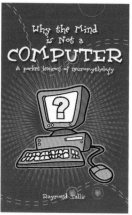

The equation 'Mind = Machine' is false. This pocket lexicon of 'neuromythology' shows why. Taking a series of keywords such as calculation, language, information and memory, Professor Tallis shows how their misuse has a misled a generation. First of all these words were used literally in the description of the human mind. Then computer scientists applied them metaphorically to the workings of machines. And finally the use of the terms was called as evidence of artificial intelligence in machines *and* the computational nature of thought.

'A splendid exception to the helpless specialisation of our age' **Mary Midgley**, *THES*

'A work of radical clarity.' *J. Consciousness Studies*

£8.95/$17.90, 9780907845942 (pbk), *Societas* V.13

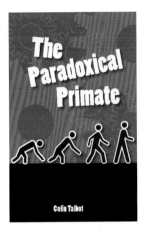

The Paradoxical Primate
Colin Talbot

This book seeks to explain how human beings can be so malleable, yet have an inherited set of instincts. When E.O. Wilson's *Consilience* made a plea for greater integration, it was assumed that the traffic would be from physical to human science. Talbot reverses this assumption and reviews some of the most innovative developments in evolutionary psychology, ethology and behavioural genetics.

'Talbot's ambition is admirable…a framework that can simultaneously encompass individualism and concern for collective wellbeing.' *Public* (The Guardian)

£8.95/$17.90, 9780907845850 (pbk), *Societas* V.14

Tony Blair and the Ideal Type
J.H. Grainger

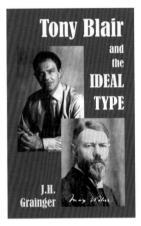

The 'ideal type' is Max Weber's hypothetical leading democratic politician, whom the author finds realized in Tony Blair. He is a politician emerging from no obvious mould, treading no well-beaten path to high office, and having few affinities of tone, character or style with his predecessors. He is the Outsider or Intruder, not belonging to the 'given' of British politics and dedicated to its transformation. (The principles outlined are also applicable. across the parties, in the post-Blair period.) The author was reader in political science at the Australian National University and is the author of *Character and Style in English Politics* (CUP).

'A brilliant essay.' **Simon Jenkins**, *Sunday Times*
'A scintillating case of the higher rudeness.' *Guardian*

£8.95/$17.90, 9781845400248 (pbk), *Societas* V.15

The Great Abdication
Alex Deane

According to Deane, Britain's middle class has abstained from its responsibility to uphold societal values, resulting in the collapse of our society's norms and standards. The middle classes must reinstate themselves as arbiters of morality, be unafraid to judge their fellow men, and follow through with the condemnation that follows when individuals sin against common values.

'[Deane] thinks there is still an element in the population which has traditional middle-class values. Well, maybe.' **George Wedd**, *Contemporary Review*

£8.95/$17.90, 9780907845973 (pbk), *Societas* V.16

Who's Afraid of a European Constitution?

Neil MacCormick

This book discusses how the EU Constitution was drafted, whether it promised any enhancement of democracy in the EU and whether it implied that the EU is becoming a superstate. The arguments are equally of interest regarding the EU Reform Treaty.

Sir Neil MacCormick is professor of public law at Edinburgh University. He was an MEP and a member of the Convention on the Future of Europe.

£8.95/$17.90, 9781845392 (pbk), *Societas* V.17

Darwinian Conservatism

Larry Arnhart

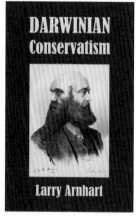

The Left has traditionally assumed that human nature is so malleable, so perfectible, that it can be shaped in almost any direction. Conservatives object, arguing that social order arises not from rational planning but from the spontaneous order of instincts and habits. Darwinian biology sustains conservative social thought by showing how the human capacity for spontaneous order arises from social instincts and a moral sense shaped by natural selection. The author is professor of political science at Northern Illinois University.

'Strongly recommended.' *Salisbury Review*

'An excellent book.' **Anthony Flew**, *Right Now!*

'Conservative critics of Darwin ignore Arnhart at their own peril.' *Review of Politics*

96 pp., £8.95/$17.90, 9780907845997 (pbk.), *Societas,* Vol. 18

Doing Less With Less: Making Britain More Secure

Paul Robinson

Notwithstanding the rhetoric of the 'war on terror', the world is now a far safer place. However, armed forces designed for the Cold War encourage global interference through pre-emption and other forms of military interventionism. We would be safer with less. The author, an ex-army officer, is assistant director of the Centre for Security Studies at Hull University.

'Robinson's criticisms need to be answered.'
Tim Garden, *RUSI Journal*

'The arguments in this thesis should be acknowledged by the MOD.' **Major General Patrick Cordingley DSO**

£8.95/$17.90, 9781845400422 (pbk), *Societas* V.19

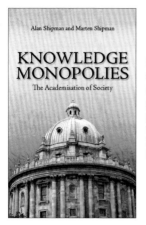

Knowledge Monopolies
Alan Shipman & Marten Shipman

Historians and sociologists chart the *consequences* of the expansion of knowledge; philosophers of science examine the *causes*. This book bridges the gap. The focus is on the paradox whereby, as the general public becomes better educated to live and work with knowledge, the 'academy' increases its intellectual distance, so that the nature of reality becomes more rather than less obscure.

'A deep and searching look at the successes and failures of higher education.' *Commonwealth Lawyer*

'A must read.' *Public* (The Guardian)

£8.95/$17.90, 9781845400286 (pbk), *Societas* V.20

The Referendum Roundabout
Kieron O'Hara

A lively and sharp critique of the role of the referendum in modern British politics. The 1975 vote on Europe is the lens to focus the subject, and the controversy over the referendum on the European constitution is also in the author's sights.

The author is a senior research fellow at the University of Southampton and author of *Plato and the Internet*, *Trust: From Socrates to Spin* and *After Blair: Conservatism Beyond Thatcher* (2005).

£8.95/$17.90, 9781845400408 (pbk), *Societas* V.21

The Moral Mind
Henry Haslam

The reality and validity of the moral sense took a battering in the last century. Materialist trends in philosophy, the decline in religious faith, and a loosening of traditional moral constraints added up to a shift in public attitudes, leaving many people aware of a questioning of moral claims and uneasy with a world that has no place for the morality. Haslam shows how important the moral sense is to the human personality and exposes the weakness in much current thinking that suggests otherwise.

'Marking a true advance in the discussion of evolutionary explanations of morality, this book is highly recommended for all collections.'
David Gordon, *Library Journal*

'An extremely sensible little book. It says things that are really rather obvious, but which have somehow got forgotten.' **Mary Midgley**

£8.95/$17.90, 9781845400163 (pbk), *Societas* V.22

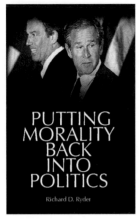

Putting Morality Back Into Politics *Richard D. Ryder*

Ryder argues that the time has come for public policies to be seen to be based upon moral objectives. Politicians should be expected routinely to justify their policies with open moral argument. In Part I, Ryder sketches an overview of contemporary political philosophy as it relates to the moral basis for politics, and Part 2 suggests a way of putting morality back into politics, along with a clearer emphasis upon scientific evidence. Trained as a psychologist, the author has also been a political lobbyist, mostly in relation to animal welfare.

£8.95/$17.90, 9781845400477 (pbk), *Societas* V.23

Village Democracy
John Papworth

'A civilisation that genuinely reflects all that human beings long for and aspire to can only be created on the basis of each person's freely acknowledged power to decide on each of the many questions that affect his life.' In the forty years since he wrote those words in the first issue of his journal *Resurgence*, John Papworth has not wavered from that belief. This latest book passionately restates his argument for radical decentralisation.

'If we are to stand any chance of surviving we need to heed Papworth's call for decentralisation.'
Zac Goldsmith, *The Ecologist*

£8.95/$17.90, 9781845400644 (pbk), *Societas* V.24

Debating Humanism
Dolan Cummings (ed.)

Broadly speaking, the humanist tradition is one in which it is we as human beings who decide for ourselves what is best for us, and are responsible for shaping our own societies. For humanists, then, debate is all the more important, not least at a time when there is discussion about the unexpected return of religion as a political force. This collection of essays follows the Institute of Ideas' inaugural 2005 Battle of Ideas festival. Contributors include Josie Appleton, Simon Blackburn, Robert Brecher, Andrew Copson, Dylan Evans, Revd. Anthony Freeman, Frank Furedi, A.C. Grayling, Dennis Hayes, Elisabeth Lasch-Quinn, Kenan Malik and Daphne Patai.

£8.95/$17.90, 9781845400699 (pbk), *Societas* V.25

The Right Road to
Radical Freedom

Tibor R. Machan

The Right Road to Radical Freedom *Tibor R. Machan*

This work focuses on the topic of free will – do we as individual human beings choose our conduct, at least partly independently, freely? He comes down on the side of libertarians who answer Yes, and scorns the compatibilism of philosophers like Daniel Dennett, who try to rescue some kind of freedom from a physically determined universe. From here he moves on to apply his belief in radical freedom to areas of life such as religion, politics, and morality, tackling subjects as diverse as taxation, private property, justice and the welfare state.

£8.95/$17.90, 9781845400187 (pbk), *Societas* V.26

Paradoxes of Power: Reflections on the Thatcher Interlude

Sir Alfred Sherman

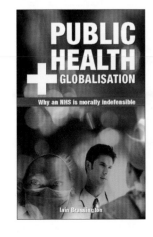

Paradoxes
of Power

Reflections on the
Thatcher Interlude

Alfred Sherman

In her memoirs Lady Thatcher herself pays tribute to her former adviser's 'brilliance', the 'force and clarity of his mind', his 'breadth of reading and his skills as a ruthless polemicist'. She credits him with a central role in her achievements. Born in 1919 in London's East End, until 1948 Sherman was a Communist and fought in the Spanish Civil War. But he ended up a free-market crusader.

'These reflections by Thatcherism's inventor are necessary reading.' **John Hoskyns**, *Salisbury Review*

£8.95/$17.90, 9781845400927 (pbk), *Societas* V.27

Public Health & Globalisation

Iain Brassington

PUBLIC
HEALTH
+ GLOBALISATION

Why an NHS is morally indefensible

Iain Brassington

This book claims that the NHS is morally indefensible. There is a good moral case in favour of a *public* health service, but these arguments do not point towards a *national* health service, but to something that looks far more like a *transnational* health service. Drawing on Peter Singer's famous arguments in favour of a duty of rescue, the author argues that the cost of the NHS is unjustifiable. If we accept a duty to save lives when the required sacrifice is small, then we ought also to accept sacrifices in the NHS in favour of foreign aid. This does not imply that the NHS is wrong; just that it is wrong to spend large amounts on one person in Britain when we could save more lives elsewhere.

£8.95/$17.90, 9781845400798 (pbk), *Societas* V.28

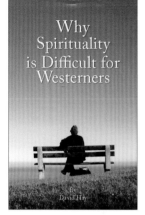

Why Spirituality is Difficult for Westerners *David Hay*

Zoologist David Hay holds that religious or spiritual awareness is biologically natural to the human species and has been selected for in organic evolution because it has survival value. Although naturalistic, this hypothesis is not intended to be reductionist. Indeed, it implies that all people have a spiritual life. This book describes the historical and economic context of European secularism, and considers recent developments in neurophysiology of the brain as it relates to religious experience.

£8.95/$17.90, 9781845400484 (pbk), *Societas* V.29

Earthy Realism: The Meaning of GAIA
Mary Midgley (ed.)

GAIA, named after the ancient Greek mother-goddess, is the notion that the Earth and the life on it form an active, self-maintaining whole. It has a *scientific* side, as shown by the new university departments of earth science which bring biology and geology together to study the continuity of the cycle. It also has a visionary or *spiritual* aspect. What the contributors to this book believe is needed is to bring these two angles together. With global warming now an accepted fact, the lessons of GAIA have never been more relevant and urgent. Foreword by James Lovelock.

£8.95/$17.90, 9781845400804 (pbk), *Societas* V.30

Joseph Conrad Today
Kieron O'Hara

This book argues that the novelist Joseph Conrad's work speaks directly to us in a way that none of his contemporaries can. Conrad's scepticism, pessimism, emphasis on the importance and fragility of community, and the difficulties of escaping our history are important tools for understanding the political world in which we live. He is prepared to face a future where progress is not inevitable, where actions have unintended consequences, and where we cannot know the contexts in which we act. The result can hardly be called a political programme, but Conrad's work is clearly suggestive of a sceptical conservatism of the sort described by the author in his 2005 book *After Blair: Conservatism Beyond Thatcher*.

£8.95/$17.90, 9781845400668 (pbk.), *Societas* V.31